Trademark Acknowledgement

ISBN: 1-4392-1215-5

Table of Contents

Table of Contents

Table of Contents

http://www.commvault.com/training

Preface

This book is designed to provide an in-depth look into storage management within CommVault® software, in particular, storage policy design. It is designed for readers with all levels of experience and should provide insight into design and implementation strategies for beginners and experts alike.

This book is NOT designed as a step-by-step how to guide. Instead, it focuses on design philosophies and concepts to make your environment work better and smarter. For step-by-step instructions for configuring features and settings, go to http://documentation.commvault.com.

CommVault also provides e-learning and instructor led training programs. You can get more information on in-depth training at http://www.commvault.com/training.

Organization of this Book

The book is divided into two sections. The first section focuses on key concepts such as storage policies, retention, and advanced features. It provides in-depth discussions and examples to help you understand how and why CommVault works the way it does. The second section is a series of design concepts which illustrate the implementations of storage policies and features to provide sound business solutions for protected data.

For **readers new to CommVault® software** it is recommended that you get comfortable using the CommCell® Console. Many features discussed in the book on a conceptual level will need to be applied through the GUI interface. This book does not provide step-by-step instructions for configuring settings within the GUI.

For **business decision makers** this book can provide excellent insight into product solutions. Whether you are currently using the product or are deciding if its right for you, this book can assist greatly in understanding all that CommVault software can do for your organization.

For **experienced CommVault software users** this book can clarify areas of confusion by providing in-depth explanations of concepts and features of the product. It can also provide insight into how you can configure your protected environment to work better.

CommVault® Software Summary of Features

CommVault Simpana® software features discussed in this book may or may not be available based on version and licensing. The following chart illustrates the version availability and licensing requirements for different features.

Feature	Feature Available in 6.1	Feature Available in 7.0	Feature Requires Additional License
Managed Disk Space	YES	YES	YES
Single Instancing	NO	YES	YES
GridStor™ feature failover & load balancing	YES	YES	YES
Synthetic Full	YES	YES	NO
Data Path Override	YES	YES	NO
Online encryption	YES	YES	YES
Offline encryption	NO	YES	YES
Extended retention	YES	YES	NO
Multistream subclient data	YES	YES	NO
Magnetic spooling	YES	YES	NO
Incremental Storage Policy	YES	YES	NO

Part I CommVault® Design and Strategy Concepts

The first part of this book will focus concepts of storage policies, data movement, retention, and planning a storage policy design strategy. Due to the cyclic nature of the Simpana® product suite, all chapters should be studied in order to gain a thorough understanding of how all the concepts come together. The final chapter in Part One will tie together all concepts into a methodology which can be used to design storage policies in a real world environment.

Chapter 1

Storage Concepts and CommVault® Architecture

Chapter Summary
- Evolution of data protection
- Business requirements for data protection
- Concepts of CommVault data management
- CommVault® software architecture
- Approaching storage policy design

In order to understand the philosophy regarding storage management we need to understand how and why we protect data, traditional backup methods, and the CommVault philosophy for data management.

Modern management of protected data is much more complicated then in previous times. Everything from documents, e-mails, databases, and even phone conversations and video surveillance is being digitized and stored. Though the capacity to store and transmit data has greatly increased, the philosophy of managing this data in the backup environment has for the most part remained the same. Most data protection software simply backs up server data and manages it based on physical locations. Using CommVault® software, intelligent, logical management of data is possible to meet a variety of business needs.

The term "*Business Needs*" will be used extensively in this book. It is important to understand that any technical decisions regarding data storage should always be based on business needs and not technical biases or legacy methodology. CommVault Simpana® software adds greater flexibility to the management of business information.

Evolution of Data Protection

Data protection has evolved considerably throughout the years. When data was managed centrally through proprietary mainframe and midrange computer systems, data could easily be protected in a consolidated backup environment. As microcomputers became more common, data protection became more complex due to the separation of data on many computer systems. As faster network bandwidth became available, it again became possible to centrally consolidate and manage backup data.

Backup software followed the evolution starting with centralized backup software. As backups became decentralized, so did backup software. Software was installed individually on each computer system requiring protection. This added great complexity to data management. With higher bandwidth and larger tape backup systems, data could again be consolidated, however most backup software was simply modified to meet changing needs.

CommVault Simpana® software was designed from the bottom up to be a true enterprise data management software suite. It allows data to be managed in a centralized or decentralized environment with a common interface for managing all protected information.

An evolutionary design in backup software emerged with the concept of policy driven data management. The idea of managing data based on business needs rather then physical placement of data on a server allowed backup engineers to design robust storage solutions. CommVault software implements this design strategy through the use of *Storage Policies*. A storage policy allows data to be logically centralized and managed based on storage and retention needs regardless of whether the data itself is physically centralized or decentralized. This provides the freedom to manage data in an infinite number of possibilities. Though this may seem like a complex method for managing backup data, the using a singular and intuitive interface for data management simplifies the complex tasks of managing protected data. CommVault software provides flexibility to meet all of today's and tomorrow's business needs providing data backup, data archiving, snapshot technology, and data replication solutions through a common management interface.

Business Reasons for Protecting Data

The reasons we protect data will vary for different companies. Though every company may have their own unique reasons for protecting business data, the underlying, basic reasons can be classified into the following categories:

- Disaster Recovery
- Data Recovery
- Data Archiving

Disaster Recovery

From a server crashing, to site loss, to major disasters affecting entire cities, it is critical to protect data based on perceived risk. Someone living in Seattle may be worried about an earthquake or a volcano eruption, while someone in the Midwest may feel tornados are the biggest problem. Identifying potential risks allows you to properly plan for a disaster. With all critical business systems, two numbers must be generated to properly prepare for a disaster:

- Recovery Time Objective (RTO)
- Recovery Point Objective (RPO)

Recovery Time Objective

RTO is the time it takes to recover from the point a critical business system is no longer available. These numbers should not be based on recovery of all systems; instead business systems should be prioritized and RTO numbers should be established based on the order in which you need to recover these systems.

Example: A file server crashes and users loose access to home folders, you may require a 48 hour time to recover. However, a critical database which is responsible for orders processing which, if down may cause your company to go out of business, may have a four hour time to recover.

Of course everyone in your company may think their system is the most critical. Your CFO may need Accounts Receivable up first to ensure revenue continues. Your CEO may want e-mail up first so he can monitor the recovery. Your CIO may want the DNS server up first because without it, none of the systems can communicate with each other. So when determining your RTO, be sure to factor in both technical dependencies and business requirements.

Recovery Point Objective

The RPO defines your acceptable amount of data loss measured in time based on business systems. If you send tapes off-site on a weekly basis you have an RPO of 7 days. The RPO, like the RTO, should always be based on business requirements. Losing 7 days of user data may not cause you to go out of business but losing just 1 hour of your orders database may result in millions of dollars of lost revenue. Even more critical will be customer confidence and public relations problems when ordered merchandise never shows up.

No business decision maker would accept data loss if there was not a cost involved. Though you can attain a near zero RPO using replication or redundant systems it will come at a great cost and there will always be a risk of some data loss. The Recovery Point Objective should be based on realistic expectations, perceived risk, and budget limitations.

Data Recovery

Disaster recovery has traditionally been the main reason we backup data but the ability to recover user data at a more granular level is extremely important as well. Let's say your sales manager is working on a huge proposal which can double your company's revenue almost overnight. The proposal documents are lost or become corrupt and they are asking you to recover them. Unfortunately the most recent backup has been sent off-site and it will take 24 hours to bring it back. By that time your company loses the deal to a competitor. For this reason, Service Level Agreements or an SLA should be set defining the acceptable length of time to recover user data.

It is recommended to always have at least two additional copies of your critical production data available at all times. One copy should be stored offsite for use during disaster recovery. The other copy should be kept local for accessibility of data restoration.

Backup Data Archiving

Because of compliance and government regulations, companies must maintain copies of financial data and communications such as e-mail and legal documents. This data usually needs to be kept for long periods of time. Just as you need to keep your personal tax records, your company needs to hold onto their records in case they are requested by government or legal entities.

Financial data usually has requirements defined to take a point-in-time backup every fiscal boundary (month, quarter, year) and archived for later recovery if necessary. Should problems arise, these records can be recovered and the company's fiscal responsibilities and reporting validated.

E-mail correspondence should also be archived. This may be easier with some e-mail applications then others. There are various methods to protecting e-mail from database backups to journaling. Looking beyond the backup method, companies need to consider what e-mail needs to be retained, how the content of those e-mails can be searched, and how easy it is to restore those e-mails. Money and time saved performing backups in a certain manner may well be insignificant when compared to the cost of restoring the data.

A private company performing database backups of an e-mail system was asked to provide all e-mails between two employees by a judge due to a sexual harassment lawsuit. The e-mails were protected in numerous database backups and scattered on many tapes. The judge required the information to be provided to the court within a specified period of time. The company did not have the manpower or time to perform the request so they had to hire a third party company to do the job. The job ended up costing over $150,000.

The point here is when most people think of e-mail archiving they think that only large public companies and government agencies need to do this. The reality is that even smaller companies have a risk and should be archiving e-mail in the most cost effective manner.

Concepts of CommVault® Data Management

CommVault software uses *Storage Policies* to define and manage the lifecycle of protected data. By using centralized policies to manage data; disaster recovery, data recovery, and compliance needs can all be met.

In traditional environments, storage administrators would create a backup of a server and then *'Clone Copy'* data to tape for off site storage. This method was adequate for linear backup strategies, but limited the ability to manage data based on business needs, instead binding the data to media based on which server it resided. Storage policies work differently by allowing the administrator to define protected data logically based on business requirements and not physical locations. This can also be thought of as *Three Dimensional* data management. It allows for better media management, improved backup performance, easier recovery, and more flexible retention strategies.

Figure 1-1: Traditional backups to tape and clone copy

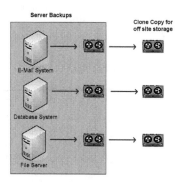

Figure 1-2: Logical management of business data using CommVault storage policies

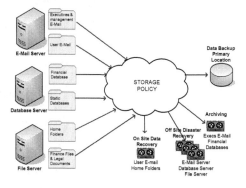

Three Dimensional Data Management

The concept of Three Dimensional data management allows for data to be protected, copied, and managed logically. Data is backed up from the production environment only once, and then additional copies can be created for off-site storage. This is based on the traditional clone copy concept. This provides a sound disaster recovery strategy by providing multiple copies to be managed independently. The backup of data is considered the *First Dimension* and the additional copy of the data for off-site storage is considered the *Second Dimension*.

The Third Dimension takes traditional data storage to the next level. It provides the ability to logically manage data independent of its physical location. Logical management of business data is accomplished by grouping production data into logical units called *subclients*. Each subclient becomes a managed object within the CommVault protected environment allowing you to customize the protection of the subclient data regardless of which physical server it originated from.

Figure 1-3: *Three dimensional storage policy providing the logical management of data based on business retention and storage needs*

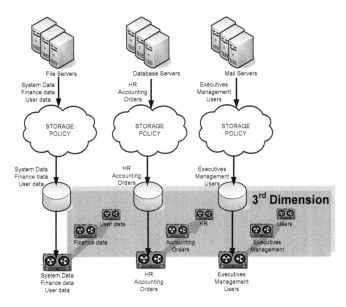

CommVault® Software Architecture

CommVault software requires the coordination of the CommServe® server, Media Agents, Libraries, and Clients. It is important to understand what each of these components do and how they interact in order to gain an overall picture of how CommVault software works.

CommServe® Server

The CommServe® server is the central management software component of a CommCell® deployment. It can be installed on Windows Server level software and hardware. The CommServe system is responsible for scheduling jobs, communicating with resources such as Clients and Media Agents, and maintaining a metadata database of all activities. It is the essential component required for all functionality and communication must be established and maintained with other components for operations to work properly.

Media Agent

The Media Agent is the high performance data mover. It is a software component that can be installed on most operating systems and platforms. All of its tasks are directed and coordinated by the CommServe server. The Media Agent moves data from a Client to a Library during a protected storage operation or vice-versa during data recovery.

Rule: With the exception of NDMP data, all data must travel through a Media Agent to reach its destination.

The rule is important to know because it will affect Media Agent placement.

Example: A Database server maintains several terabytes of data located in a Storage Area Network (SAN). The backup location for the data is also in the SAN. Server to Server communication is via the LAN so database backups to a Media Agent will require the data to be sent to a Media Agent over the LAN and then back into the SAN to the storage media.

Solution: By placing a Media Agent module on the same host as the database server, the data can be managed internally within the server and written directly into the SAN. This is called a LAN free backup.

Figure 1-4: *Diagram of a LAN based backup (left) and a LAN-Free backup (right)*

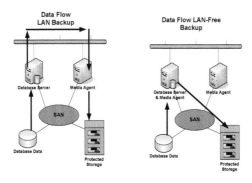

Libraries

Removable media library

The most common method of storing data off-site is by using removable media libraries. The most common removable media library is a tape library, but optical disks, or USB drives can also be used to protect data. CommVault software treats each removable piece of media as unique storage and allows the transparent recovery of data from such media from any compatible library within the *CommCell* architecture.

Magnetic library

Magnetic libraries take advantage of multi-stream, high speed, random access magnetic disks for data storage. Magnetic libraries are configured by defining *mount paths* to the data volumes/disks. A mount path can be defined by a local drive letter and or folder, SAN volume, or network path. Mount paths can be unique to a library or shared using shared file systems, SCSI connections, or network protocols. While a single mount path can be defined for a library, multiple mount paths taking advantage of different I/O channels is recommended. Mount paths can be added dynamically as more space is required.

Client

A client is defined as a production server running CommVault client agent software designed to protect distinct data types managed by a server. As with Media Agents, Client tasks are managed and coordinated by the CommServe system.

CommCell® Architecture

A CommCell® deployment defines the management boundaries of all CommVault components under the control of a single CommServe server. The CommServe system will coordinate all tasks and data movement with the CommCell environment.

Figure 1-5: Diagram of a simple CommCell deployment with a CommServe server, Client, Media Agent, and a tape library

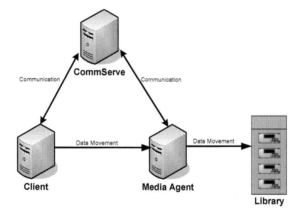

iDataAgent

Each Client server requiring protection will have at least one *iDataAgent* installed. All major operating systems are supported by CommVault.

iDataAgent software support:
- File system agents
- Application database agents
- Application object/document level agents

Backup Set

A *Backup Set* is a logical restore view of all protected data for which an iDataAgent is responsible. For instance; a backup set for a file system iDataAgent will represent every drive, folder, and file (except mapped network drives) on a server. Most iDataAgents will have a *Default Backup Set* Additional backup sets can be configured if needed, but may result in production data being backed up multiple times.

Subclient

A subclient is the smallest logical management container representing production data. Each backup set will have at least one subclient (*default*) preconfigured. The default subclient will represent all data within a file system or application that is not otherwise defined within another subclient. This means that data contained in subclients within a backup set will not be backed up more then once using normal schedule settings.

Figure 1-6: *File System iDataAgent defining data within several subclients contained within a backup set. All data on the file server will be backed up through the Default subclient except the folder locations defined in the Home Folders and Finance subclients*

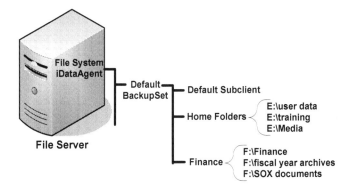

Approaching Storage Policy Design

In order to understand storage policies and CommVault design strategies, the philosophy and methodology of working with storage policies must be explained. The breakdown of storage policy concepts covered in this book are:

How Storage Policies work

Understanding how storage policies work will help to understand the key concepts of policy design. This will include primary and secondary copies as well as understanding the way CommVault software manages data in the backup environment.

Data Movement Process

Once we understand the logical makeup of storage policies we need to understand how the data is moved to the backup environment. This chapter will provide a thorough understanding of data streams, backup performance, moving data to secondary copies, and auxiliary copy operations.

Retention and Data Lifecycle Management

The key aspect of retention is to determine business needs and implement retention strategies to meet those needs. CommVault software's retention methodology complements business needs rather than forcing business needs to fit the technology. This chapter will focus on both of these key aspects.

Information Lifecycle Management

This chapter will expand on the concepts of data management and retention by explaining how CommVault software can be used to implement ILM strategies. Information Lifecycle Management allows the archiving and management of data based on the type of data and the ownership of that data. This breaks the traditional bounds of data management based on physical server location or folder structures.

Advanced CommVault Concepts

To fully appreciate the power and flexibility of storage policies, advanced features and concepts will need to be explained. These features will be covered to provide a general understanding of how they work. Understanding these features will be crucial to gaining a full understanding of the power and flexibility of CommVault software.

Implementing Storage Policies

Implementing storage policies will tie together all key concepts of storage policy design and implementation. It will provide a consolidated approach to designing and implementing policies. Once the basic concepts of CommVault features are understood, this chapter can be used as a reference point when designing storage policies in your real world production environment.

CommVault® Software Solutions and Examples

The second part of the book will focus on implementations of storage policies and CommVault software features in real world scenarios. Many of these examples have been used in actual environments to simplify data management, meet business needs, and reduce total cost of ownership. These examples will include a complete case study for a ground up policy strategy design, and individual strategies which can be used to improve existing environments.

Design examples will be broken into: storage policy case study, basic storage policy examples, advanced examples, distributed environment examples, enterprise examples and disaster recovery examples. To best use this section, read through the case study to get a basic idea of how strategies are designed and implemented. Once you have the basic concepts down in the case study, you can apply individual solutions as explained in the last four chapters of the book.

Summary

Many organizations decide to use the CommVault Simpana suite in their environments for a few essential features, platform support, reliability, ease of use, or its quality of support. Few organizations have yet to take full advantage of all the power and flexibility of the product. Many customers that I have talked to only scratch the surface of the true capabilities of CommVault software. This book is designed to explain and illustrate the full power of the Simpana product suite.

I hope that in writing this book, not only will technical users gain a more thorough understanding of the product, but that this book also will be used as a guide for non-technical decision makers within an organization. Because of that reason, much of this book will focus on business reasons for protecting data. Many tables and charts will be used which can form the basis of building a complete data protection strategy.

Whether or not you take advantage of the full potential of CommVault software solutions, it is important to understand all of the capabilities it can provide. It is also important to understand that as your organization grows, you will already have a robust data management solution in place to meet to meet any needs that may arise.

Chapter 2

How a Storage Policy Works

Chapter Summary
- Conceptual overview
- Defining the data path
- Storage policy copies
- Storage policy best practices

A storage policy defines the data lifecycle management rules for protected data. In its most basic form, a storage policy can be thought of as a container. This container will be used to manage protected data. Within a storage policy multiple policy copies can be defined. Each copy will contain rules defining how data will be managed within the copy. These rules are applied to the policy copy based on business and technical reasons for protecting the data as defined by your company. The basic rules contained within each storage policy copy will be what data will be managed by the policy, how long will the data be kept for, and where the data will be managed by the copy.

The key aspect of CommVault® storage policies is to move data from the production environment into the protected environment. Once data is in the protected environment it is no longer bound to its originating physical location. This allows the data to be managed as logical units. These logical units can be grouped or separated regardless of the platform or application they originated from. The flexibility gained from policy driven data protection and management is the ability to group data based on protection and retention needs greatly simplifying the organization and management of protected data.

Figure 2-1: *A storage policy represented as a container. Within the container are multiple copies to define data lifecycle management rules for each copy*

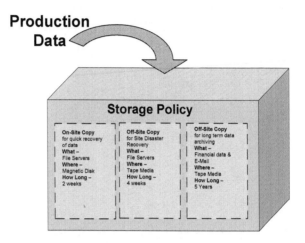

The diagram in figure 2-1 shows a storage policy represented as a container with multiple copies within it. CommVault software typically uses a cloud to represent a storage policy. To remain consistent with CommVault training and documentation, this book will use clouds to represent all storage policies diagrams.

Figure 2-2: *Storage policy represented as a cloud*

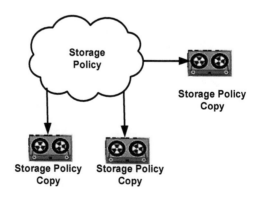

It is important to understand that a storage policy defines rules for how data will be managed. Moving the data into the storage policy and from one copy to another will be done through scheduling mechanisms such as schedule policies and auxiliary copy operations. Chapter three will focus on the movement of data from one copy to another. This chapter will focus on the components of a storage policy and how they are configured.

In managing protected data there are several tasks a storage policy performs:

- Creates logical divisions of business data
- Facilitates the movement of data from the production environment into protected storage
- Updates and maintains multiple copies of the data for various business needs
- Manages content, retention, and validation for data within each copy

Logical Divisions of Business Data

Storage policies facilitate the ease of movement and management of protected data. In addition to the primary protected copy, additional copies can be created within the storage policy to further divide and manage data. Each storage policy copy independently manages the data assigned to it. Business requirements for protected storage such as; how long to keep the data, what data will be copied, encryption, data verification, and where the data will be stored are all managed within a storage policy copy.

Figure 2-3: *A storage policy with three policy copies. Each copy independently owns and manages data associated within the copy*

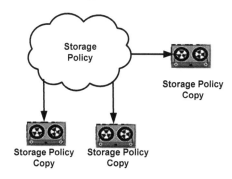

A storage policy creates logical boundaries that should be based on business requirements within an organization. Data associated with and managed by a storage policy is bound to that storage policy. Data can be moved between copies within the same storage policy, but data cannot be moved to a different storage policy.

> Since CommVault software logically manages all protected data through storage policies it is **absolutely critical** to understand that if a policy is deleted, all associated data will be unrecoverable through the *CommCell®️ Console*. Storage policies containing retained data should not be deleted. You can use the job history view to determine if data is still being managed by a policy. If it is, consider renaming the policy. For example: SP_Win_Servers can be renamed X_SP_Win_Serv-123108. 123108 can represent the data in which all data will be aged from the policy and at that point it can be deleted. NOTE: you can change the name of a storage policy at any time.
>
> If you do delete a storage policy you can recover data by restoring a previous DR backup prior to the storage policy's deletion or by using the Media Explorer tool. Refer to the CTE Desktop Reference book or CommVault documentation for more information on using Media Explorer.

Defining the Data Path

Subclients point to storage policies which define the data path from the Media Agent to protected storage. Data paths can be customized for each storage policy copy and multiple data paths can be defined for a single storage policy. This allows for several key advantages:

- Distributed environments in multiple locations can use multiple storage policies to define local paths for protected data.
- File and application servers backing up over the LAN can use storage policies that can be configured to load balance or failover between multiple paths.
- Servers with SAN attached storage can be configured to perform LAN free backups.
- Defining multiple paths within a storage policy allows you to use fewer storage policies.

The data path if made up of four parts:

1. Media Agent
2. Library
3. Drive pool
4. Scratch pool

Media Agent

Media Agents are the workhorses that move data from production servers to the backup environment. They supply the processing power to receive data, arrange it in chunk format, and send it to the library. Media Agents can also be responsible for encryption, compression, or hash generation for single instance storage. Multiple Media Agents can be used to write to a multi stream capable library to improve overall performance by load balancing jobs across multiple paths and/or devices.

Figure 2-4: Multiple Media Agents writing to a four drive tape library using round-robin load balancing

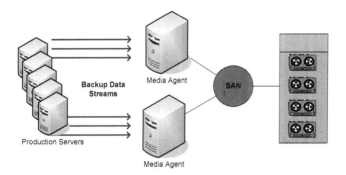

Library

Libraries are logically defined and are categorized as stationary or removable media libraries. Stationary libraries define a path to a magnetic disk location such as a drive letter or UNC path. They are considered stationary since these paths cannot change once defined. Magnetic (disk) libraries provide advantages over traditional tape libraries since more streams can be written simultaneously increasing the aggregate throughput and data can be managed and moved easier on disk as opposed to tape.

Removable media libraries are generally thought of as tape libraries but they can also be magnetic optical or USB storage devices. The advantage of removable media libraries is that media can be moved between libraries and recognized by CommVault software to be restored. Capacity can also be inexpensively added by simply adding more media to the library. Traditionally, removable media was the only option for off-site storage but with disk replication and higher bandwidth becoming relatively affordable this is starting to change.

Drive Pool

Drive pools are a single Media Agents view of allocated drives within a removable media library. Use of drive pools gives the Media Agent the flexibility of drive choice and usage within a library. Without drive pools, assigning and sending a data protection job to a specific drive will fail if the drive is broken or offline. Having a pool of drives to choose from gives the job the best chance of success.

With multiple Media Agents using the same library, each Media Agent has its own logical drive pool view of the physical drives. This allows each Media Agent to use any of the drives for reading/writing data. Note that not all physical drives need to be allocated or made available in each Media Agent's Drive pool. Restricting the number of drives assigned or allocated to each Media Agent's Drive pool is a load balancing feature to prevent a Media Agent from becoming saturated with data movement streams which can result in poor performance or failure of the Media Agent.

There is also a Master Drive Pool configuration available within a Library. Master Drive Pools are used to separate dissimilar drive types into different drive pools. For example; a library may have four physical drives made up of two LTO2 and two LTO4 drives. While the media written to by LTO2 drives can be read in an LTO4 drive, the opposite is not true. A Master Drive Pool enables the separation of different drive types and their respective media.

Scratch Pool

Scratch pools allow new and re-usable media within the library to be logically grouped based on media type and intended usage. At least one default scratch pool exists for every removable media library. Master Drive pools can be assigned their own default scratch pools. More, user-defined scratch pools can be created as assigned to a data path as desired.

Figure 2-5: Using drive pools and scratch pools to logically divide resources within a removable media library.

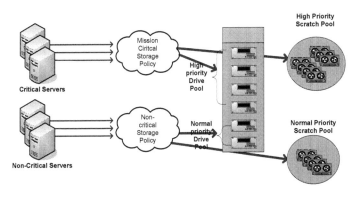

One interesting use of scratch pools is to designate a particular pool for compliance jobs. Regulations may require a job to go to a specific tape. Defining a scratch pool for compliance and then moving the tape to that pool will force CommVault software to pick that particular tape when the job is performed. To accomplish this, create a storage policy copy for the compliance job and specify the scratch pool defined for compliance in the data path.

Multiple Data Paths Using GridStor™ Technology

GridStor™ architecture provides the ability to configure multiple data paths to storage within a storage policy. Having multiple data paths enables the administrator to route data from multiple clients to storage on the best path available; re-route data should a data path resource fail or load balance data movement across the paths for performance. By defining multiple paths the number of storage policies needed within a CommCell environment can be reduced. This will make it easier to manage your backup data and help consolidate the amount of media required to protect business data.

Default Data Path

When creating a storage policy, a default path will be defined. As additional paths are added, the default path can be changed. Given no other guidance, all LAN based subclients associated with the storage policy will use the default path.

Example: You have just added a new magnetic disk library in your CommCell environment. You have an existing storage policy with a default path pointing to a tape library and you want to redirect all backup data to the new disk storage.

Solution: In the storage policy copy, add the data path to the magnetic library and select the new path as the default path.

Figure 2-6: Magnetic library replacing a tape library as the default data path

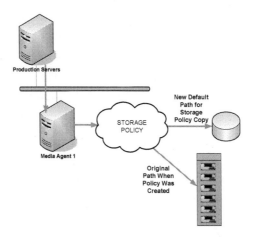

Preferred Data Path

While multiple paths are defined, the preferred path is determined by the CommVault software. A preferred path is one that uses a locally hosted (non-LAN) Media Agent. When a preferred path is available, it will always be used to move data to storage. In a preferred path configuration where the preferred path becomes unavailable, alternate paths will not be used. You can accomplish LAN-Free backups by co-locating Media Agent software on Client enabled servers.

Example: You have several servers which will be backing up over the LAN and several servers attached to the SAN. You want to use a dedicated Media Agent for LAN based backups and you want to backup any SAN attached servers using a LAN-Free backup.

Solution: By installing Media Agent software on each SAN attached server you can perform LAN-Free backups. All LAN backups will use the dedicated Media Agent.

Figure 2-7: *LAN-Free paths defined for SAN attached servers*

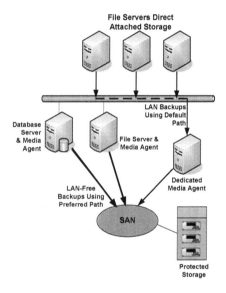

Data Path Load Balancing

In a small backup environment using one Media Agent may be adequate for all backup needs. As an environment grows multiple Media Agents may be needed to distribute or route data movement for better performance. You can define multiple paths within a storage policy copy and configure those paths to Round-Robin load balance.

Example: You have several servers backing up over the LAN. The Media Agent currently handling the backups is no longer able to move all data to the library within your backup window.

Solution: You install another Media Agent and add the data path to the storage policy copy. You configure GridStor to Round-Robin (load balance) between the paths.

Figure 2-8: two media agents used to round-robin load balance backup data for LAN backups.

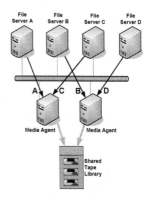

Data Path Failover

In some cases you may also want to define another path if the default path is not available. Data path failover can be used to failover to another path if the default path is unavailable or if a resource in the path is offline or unavailable.

Example: You have two Media Agents with direct attached libraries. You want a file server to backup to the magnetic library. However, if the library or Media Agent are down you want to be able to use the other Media Agent and tape library to ensure the data is protected.

Solution: Define the data path to both Media Agents. Define the magnetic library path as the default path. Configure the storage policy copy to failover to the other path if resources are off-line.

Figure 2-9: File server configured to backup to a magnetic library and to failover to a tape library if the default path becomes unavailable.

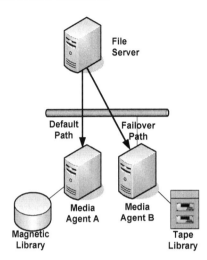

Using GridStor™ Technology for Storage Policy Consolidation

Since storage policies create logical divisions for business data it is important not to configure too many policies as each policy will require its own set of media. If you have ten storage policies assigned to a tape library and want to send data off-site every day you will be sending a minimum of ten tapes daily.

Using GridStor features to define multiple data paths allows you to consolidate the number of storage policies needed within your environment. Data can be managed centrally through a storage policy but data paths can be configured to distribute backups to the appropriate storage locations. Since the data is managed by the same policy, backup jobs can be consolidated on media for more efficient media usage.

Storage Policy Copies

A main concept of storage policies is to require the movement of data from the production environment to protected storage only once. When the data is in the backup environment, the storage policy logically manages and maintains copies of the data. This allows the flexibility of managing data based on the three key aspects of data protection: disaster recovery, data recovery, and data archiving.

There are three types of storage policy copies:

- Primary Copy
- Secondary Synchronous Copy
- Secondary Selective Copy

Primary Copies

The Primary copy of a storage policy is the first stop for backup data. Data is backed up from production servers to the primary copy location using one or more streams. Multiple streams for data protection jobs permits the parallel transfer of data from production servers to the backup environment. While the final repository of the primary copy is usually a single library, there is no requirement as such. A Primary copy with multiple paths can use any number of libraries with different media.

When backing up to the primary location the main focus is performance. You want to get production data into your backup environment as efficiently as possible. Once the data is in the backup environment it can be managed independently allowing the creation of additional copies.

Figure 2-10: Data from production environment backed up to primary location. Additional copies are then made from the primary location.

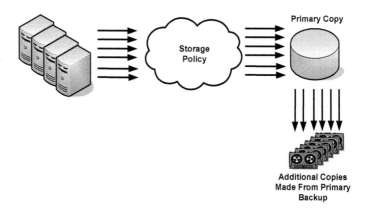

CommVault recommends using magnetic disk media for primary backups. Disks are inherently fast and allow for multiple source writes of backup streams allowing for more simultaneous backups to run. Disks can increase the overall *Aggregate Throughput* of your backup environment. Traditional tape devices are single, sequential stream devices with overhead of mounting/loading the necessary media. While they can operate at high speed they only support data originating from a single Media Agent source. Their main benefit is removability for disaster recovery.

Secondary Copies

Once data is protected to the primary copy location, additional copies can be created. Additional copies can then be generated within the backup environment without impacting the production resources. Each additional copy can be used for different purposes such as off-site DR, on-site data recovery, or off-site archiving.

Secondary copies are used to configure the following:

- Data path, or physical destination of the copy
- Retention
- What data will be copied which is accomplished through subclient associations
- Offline encryption options

There are two types of secondary copies: *Synchronous* and *Selective*

Synchronous Copy

A *synchronous copy* defines a secondary copy to synchronize backup data with a source copy. All valid data written to the source copy will be copied to the synchronous copy via an update copy process called an Auxiliary Copy operation (note: Inline copy is an Auxiliary copy operation performed simultaneously with the backup operation.) Synchronous copies are useful when you want a consistent point-in-time copy of all protected data available for restore. This will include all full, incremental, differential, and transaction log backups.

Figure 2-11: *Synchronous copies create additional copies of all Fulls, incrementals, and differentials.*

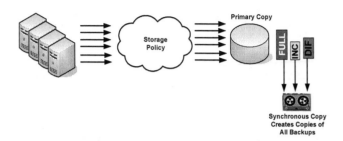

Selective Copy

A *selective copy* allows automatic selection of specific full backups or manual selection of any backup for additional protection. Selective copy options allow the time based, automatic selection of all, weekly, monthly, quarterly, half-year, and/or yearly full backups. You can also choose to manually select any backup to be copied.

Selective copies are useful for the following reasons:

- Data being sent off-site weekly, monthly, quarterly, or yearly
- Archiving point-in-time copies of data for compliance and government regulations

Figure 2-12: *Example showing a selective copy configured to take the end of the month full to create an additional copy.*

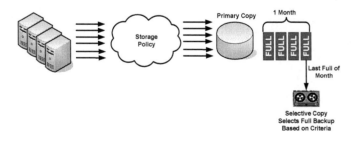

Secondary Copy Features

Secondary copies allow for great flexibility for selecting and managing data for additional copies. The following configurations can be set for secondary copies:

- Copy associations to determine which subclients will be copied
- Combine of data source streams to consolidate multiple backup streams to fewer media
- Specify source for copy if the Primary copy is not available or does not contain the necessary data
- Data encryption

Secondary Copy Associations

Determining what data will be managed by a secondary copy can be configured through *subclient associations*. Subclients are the smallest logical management unit of data within the backup environment. Each secondary copy can have unique data associated with the copy determined at the subclient level. This allows you to create additional copies for various reasons.

Example: You want to define a storage policy to allow for quick recovery of all data on a server, off-site disaster recovery, long term file recovery for user data, and long term archiving of legal documents.

Solution: A storage policy is configured with a primary copy, two synchronous copies and one selective copy. Figure 2-8 illustrates the storage policy implementation.

Figure 2-13: A storage policy with a primary and three secondary copies to accomplish data protection goals.

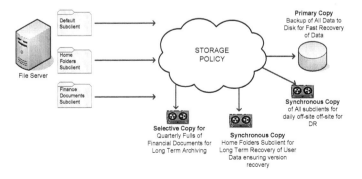

Combine to Streams

A storage policy can be configured to allow the use of multiple streams for primary copy backup. Multi-streaming of backup data is done to improve backup performance. Normally, each stream used for the Primary copy requires a corresponding stream on each secondary copy. In the case of tape media for a secondary copy, multi-stream storage policies will consume multiple media. The *combine to streams* option can be used to consolidate multiple streams from source data on to fewer media when secondary copies are run. This allows for better media management and the grouping of like data onto media for storage. The combine to streams option will be discussed in more detail in the next chapter.

Specify Source Copy

By default the source location for data to create secondary copies will be the primary location. This can be changed, however, through the *Specify Source* option in the *Copy Policy* tab within the storage policy copy.

Example: You perform daily backups to magnetic media and daily synchronous copies to tape. You then perform a weekly selective copy to tape. Disk capacity is limited and you want to keep the data only for several days but the weekly selective copy does not run until Sunday.

Solution: Specify the source copy to be the secondary synchronous to allow data to age from magnetic disk.

Figure 2-14: Daily backups are performed to disk then copies to tape. A weekly selective copy is then performed from the source, in this case tape to tape.

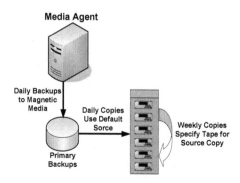

Data Encryption

Encrypting data is an essential part of data protection, especially when data is being placed on removable media. A lot of time and money is spent on front line defense to prevent intrusion into your production environment. Consideration must also be paid to backup data. If a tape is stolen with sensitive information on it, there will be no way to prevent someone from accessing that data. No firewall or highly paid security expert will be able to save your data. Even if it takes months to access the data on the tape, the information will still ultimately be compromised.

CommVault software offers three methods to encrypt data. Inline encryption will encrypt data during the backup job, offline encryption which encrypts backup data while being copied to secondary copies, or hardware encryption using LTO 4 type drives. Inline and Offline encryption is software based. Inline encryption can be performed on the Client or Media Agent. Offline encryption will be performed on the Media Agent. LTO 4 type drives support hardware encryption which is performed on the drive itself. CommVault Simpana software supports the following encryption algorithms:

Cipher	Key Length
3-DES	192
AES (Rijndael)	128 or 256
Blowfish	128 or 256
Serpent	128 or 256
TwoFish	128 or 256

The following chart illustrates how encryption can be used with CommVault software and advantages / disadvantages of each method.

Type	Where Encryption is Performed	How it is Enabled / Disabled	Advantages	Disadvantages
In-Line	Client or Media Agent	Turned on/off at subclient level	Allows encryption over network	Software based hits CPU & memory of client or Media Agent
Off-line	Media Agent	Turned on/off at storage policy secondary copy.	Does not affect primary backup windows	Software based hits CPU & memory of client or Media Agent
LTO 4	LTO 4 drive with encryption support	Turned on/off at storage policy secondary copy.	Hardware based faster encryption & no load on client or Media Agent	Requires dedicated hardware for backups and restores

With any of these encryption solutions, keys will always be stored in the CommServe® database. Optionally keys can be stored on the media as well. This can be useful when using the *Media Explorer* tool to recover data from media.

Storage Policy Best Practices

Though there is no "one size fits all" solution for designing storage policies, the following section lists some basic guidelines to assist in storage policy design.

Storage Policy Consolidation

The fewer storage policies you have the less backup fragmentation will happen. To clarify this statement, realize that backup fragmentation is not the same as file fragmentation. What is meant here is that since subclients are associated with storage policies on a one-to-one basis, data can not be combined between policies. Storage policies create logical divisions of data based on business needs.

Example: Backing up 40 clients to a tape library each to their own storage policy will result in 40 tapes being required in the library to handle all the jobs.

Solution: By consolidating the number of active storage policies your backups will require fewer media to perform backups.

When determining your storage policy design, it is critical to plan out your data storage strategies before implementing them within the interface. Setting up storage policies is the easy part, determining your storage policy design is the hard part. The chapter on implementing storage policies will focus on the overall design and implementation of storage policies.

Chapter 3

CommVault® Data Movement Process

Chapter Summary
- Understanding data streams
- Managing streams
- Optimizing backup performance
- Copying data to secondary copies

Understanding how CommVault® software moves data within the production and backup environment is essential to understanding how to configure your physical environment, the logical environment, and to help improve performance.

Understanding Data Streams

Data Streams are what CommVault software uses to move data from source to destination. The source can be production data or backup data. Configuring stream performance always starts with ensuring there is enough available bandwidth to move data and enough memory and CPU power to process the data being moved.

Data streams are divided into *Job Streams* and *Device Streams*. Job streams move data from the production environment to the Media Agent. Device streams move data from the Media Agent to storage.

Figure 3-1: Data streams divided into Job Streams and Device Streams

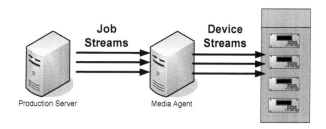

Job Streams

Job streams are used to move data from the production environment to a Media Agent. Each iDataAgent will use its own streams to move data. There are two ways you can configure streams within an iDataAgent. The first is to define multiple subclients. Each subclient represents its own job meaning each one will use its own set of streams. The other way is to increase the number of streams for an individual subclient. This is accomplished by setting the number of *Data Readers* for the subclient. The term *readers* is used because it defines the number of simultaneous read operations that will be performed from the source disks. Note that for each reader stream, a corresponding device, writer, or multiplexed stream is required on the data path.

Figure 3-2: Example of stream divisions of a production server. Each subclient represents its own stream or set of streams. Some subclients are configured to multistream backups based on the number of physical disks present.

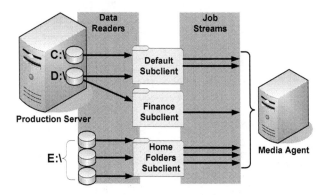

Configuring Job streams

You can define multiple subclients within a backup set to improve performance by multistreaming and stagger scheduling data protection operations when large amounts of data must be moved. Do not configure too many subclients as this can actually have a negative effect on performance. Another way to improve performance is to identify problem areas where specific data is taking too long to backup (i.e. home folders or user mailboxes) and define them as separate subclients. If the data resides on high performance disks or disk arrays, increasing the number of readers will multistream the backup job.

Data Readers

By default, the number of readers allowed for simultaneous use is based on the number of physical disks available. The limit is one reader per physical disk. If there is one physical disk with two logical partitions, setting the readers to 2 will have no effect. Having too many simultaneous read operations on a single disk could potentially cause the disk heads to thrash slowing down the backups and potentially decreasing the life of the disk.

Viewing the number of readers per job in the Job Controller
Fields in the job controller can be customized to show additional information. The fields *Number of Data Readers* and *Data Readers in Use* can be added to view the number of streams being attempted and used for each job. Refer to CommVault documentation for more information on customizing the Job Controller.

Allow multiple readers within a drive or Mount Point

When a disk array that contains several physical disks is addressed logically by the OS as a single drive letter, the *Allow multiple readers within a drive or mount point* can be used as an override. This will allow a backup job to take advantage of the fast read access of a RAID array.

Can I use the override for a single disk too?
Well, yes you can, but... consider these important points:

- Only increase the readers for a single disk if it's a high speed SCSI disk
- CommVault recommends no more than 2 readers
- Defrag the disks! Contiguously stored data is much quicker to access. Defragged disks are faster and will give you a longer life. Consider a dedicated defrag utility and don't use the OS defrag unless you have a few weeks to wait for it to finish!
- Consider other ways to improve performance such as Network Agents, using multiple subclients and stagger scheduling jobs, or moving data to faster performance disks or into the SAN (if you have one)

Device Streams

As Job Streams are received by the Media Agent, data is put into chunk format and sent out to media as *Device Streams*. Depending on configurations data may be multiplexed, encrypted, hashed for single instancing, or compressed. Data chunks are then sent to the assigned drive (removable media) or writer (magnetic media) to be written to the media.

There are several reasons that there is a distinction between job streams and device streams. First the data is sent to the Media Agent in raw format, processed and then written to media in CommVault storage format. The second reason is that job streams and device streams are not always a 1-to-1 ratio. In the case of multiplexing, multiple job streams can be written in a single device stream. Diagram 2-7 illustrates the process flow of data and configuration options which will appear in the interface to configure stream performance.

Figure 3-3: *Multiple job streams being multiplexed into device streams within the Media Agent.*

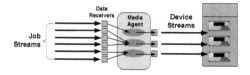

Configuring Device Streams

Device streams are configured in the properties of the storage policy. The default setting is 1. The general rule of thumb is that the number of device streams configured in a storage policy should always equal the number of drives or writers in the library. Having fewer number of streams may be used to throttle parallel throughput, but that doesn't make maximum efficient use of the devices and there are other means to restrict allocation of devices. Having more streams than devices creates the potential of orphan streams with media consumption that poses no benefit to the task at hand.

Managing Streams

Managing device streams is divided into two areas, Primary copy streams and secondary copy streams. Streams may be configured and handled differently for each type.

Primary Copy Streams

Primary copy streams are job streams. When performing primary copy backups, performance is the main goal to ensure backup windows are met. Writing to magnetic media allows for many streams to be processed and written simultaneously. When writing to removable media libraries you are limited by the number of devices (drives) available. While multiplexing will allow more streams it is not the primary purpose of multiplexing.

Multiplexing

Multiplexing allows multiple job streams flowing into a media agent to be multiplexed together into a device stream. The primary reason for multiplexing is to keep buffers of high speed tape drives filled and not simply to run more jobs.

Example: You are backing up two file servers over a switched network. There are millions of objects on each server and data is moderately fragmented. Backing up each of these servers serially to two drives may result in the backups running slower. In this case the fragmentation of the data is causing a bottleneck. This results in the Media Agent sending data to the drives below optimal speeds causing the drives to slow down for variable speed drives or to 'Shoe Shine' for fixed speed drives.

Figure 3-4: Two server backing up to two drives in parallel streams through a single media agent.

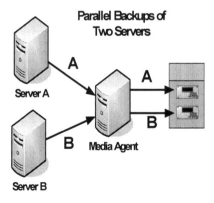

Parallel Backups of
Two Servers

Server A

A

A

Media Agent

B

B

Server B

Solution: By multiplexing incoming streams from both servers the Media Agent can feed more data to one drive and the drive will spin faster. It also frees up the other drive to perform additional backups.

Figure 3-5: Using multiplexing two servers can be multiplexed to a single drive. This improves backup performance by allowing multi-speed drives to spin faster.

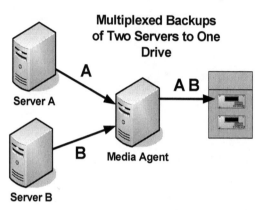

Multiplexed Backups of Two Servers to One Drive

Secondary Copy Streams

For most data centers, performance is the key requirement when performing primary backups from the production servers. When copying data to secondary copies, media management becomes the primary focus. If a backup job was conducted using 3 streams and you want to make an additional copy of that job to tape, by default those 3 streams will go onto 3 different tapes. Using the *Combine to Streams* option you can consolidate those streams onto fewer tapes.

Example: You backup a home folders subclient to a magnetic library using 3 streams to maximize performance. The total size of protected data is 600GB. You want to consolidate those 3 streams onto a single 800GB capacity tape for off-site storage.

Solution: By creating a secondary copy and setting the Combine to Streams setting to 1 you will serially place each stream onto the media.

Figure3-6: *Combine to streams setting to 1 will take streams A, B, and C and serially write them to 1 tape.*

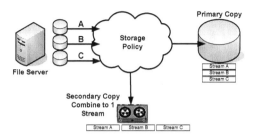

Optimizing Backup Performance

Optimizing performance always starts with the physical environment. Ensuring there is adequate network bandwidth between the production server and media agent, CPU, memory, and high performance libraries always transcend software configurations. The following section details configurations you can make to improve CommCell® environment performance.

Subclient Performance

Improving backup performance always starts with ensuring your production servers can send data fast and efficiently. Network speed, Media Agent power, and library performance means nothing if your heavily fragmented disks can not read the data fast enough to send it out.

Considerations for subclient configuration:

- Always ensure source data is contiguously stored, in other words *DEFRAG*.
- Filter out unneeded data. Refer to CommVault Books Online documentation for manufacture recommended filters for major operating systems and applications.
- If bandwidth, writers, and disk I/O allows, increasing the number of data readers will parallel backup operations by multistreaming.
- Creating multiple subclients can improve backup performance by multistreaming jobs and stagger scheduling large volume backups.
- Grouping data based on business needs provides the ability to manage that data independently in the backup environment.

Stream Performance for Libraries

Depending on whether you are using removable media or magnetic media libraries, configuration options can be used to maximize performance and media management. CommVault recommends writing data to magnetic media, but tape libraries are still very common and cost effective methods for protecting and managing data. Whichever method you use, the following section provides methods for optimizing the performance of libraries.

Magnetic vs. Removable Media Libraries

CommVault strongly recommends writing primary backup data to magnetic libraries. The inherent speed and ability to write multiple streams can make a significant improvement on backup performance. The random access of magnetic disks can also greatly increase the speed of data recovery. With new technologies such as *Single Instancing* data can be compressed with extremely high ratios making disk storage more efficient than tape.

Considerations for Magnetic Library

- Optimally configure the number of writers for each mount path
- Consider Spill & Fill (load balancing) of multiple mount paths
- If limited in disk capacity consider spooling to disk and using the spool location to stage backup data to secondary copies.

Considerations for Tape Library

- Consider using multiplexing to improve tape speed performance
- For Dynamic Drive Sharing libraries in a SAN environment consider using multiple Media Agents to balance writes when using many drives

> **What about VTL libraries?**
> Virtual Tape Libraries simulate writing to tape but actually write to disk. VTL libraries were initially designed when most backup solutions were not inherently capable of writing to disk. CommVault Simpana® software was always capable of writing to disk. Many vendors still try to push VTL solutions especially when bundled with dedicated disk hardware. Though CommVault software will work with third party VTL software, some advanced functionality may be limited by use of VTL. Also realize that you are adding an extra layer in the backup and restore process. If you are going to use VTL solutions ensure that all DR procedures take VTL issues into account.

Whenever trying to improve performance, analyze your environment as a whole and find key areas causing bottlenecks such as network, Media Agent, or libraries. Then focus in on key areas that need improving. If your environment is running well but there are a few servers not meeting backup windows, focus in on those trouble spots to improve their performance. Always realize that improving performance in one area could potentially have a negative effect in another.

NOTE: See CommVault documentation and the CTE reference book for more information on improving backup performance.

Copying Data to Secondary Copies

When you want to backup production servers you either schedule the job at the client level or through a schedule policy. In either case you choose which server you want to backup. Once data is in the backup environment it is no longer tied to the production server, instead it is managed by the storage policy. There are various methods for copying data to secondary copies. The following methods can be used to move data to secondary copies:

- Inline copy
- Auxiliary copy
  - Schedule
  - On demand
  - Save as script
  - Automatic copy

Inline Copy

The Inline Copy feature allows you to create additional copies of data at the same time you are performing primary backups. This feature can be useful when you need to get two copies of data done quickly. Data is passed from the client to the Media Agent as job streams. The Media Agent then creates two sets of device streams, each going to the appropriate library. This can be a quick method for creating multiple copies but there are some caveats:

- If the primary copy fails the secondary copy will also fail.
- Since both copies are made at the same time twice as many library resources will be required which may prevent other jobs from running.
- Since backup data is streamed, data will be sent to both libraries simultaneously, which may cause overall performance to degrade. Basically your job will run as fast as the slowest resource.

Figure 3-7: Inline copy receives two streams from the client server and sends those streams to two different libraries.

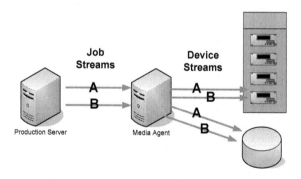

Auxiliary Copy Operations

Before discussing auxiliary copy operations, a very important distinction in terms must be made. I am referring to the difference between secondary copies and auxiliary copy operations. Secondary copies allow you to configure where the data will go (data path), how long it will stay there for (retention), and what data you want to copy (subclient associations). An *auxiliary copy operation* determines when the data will be copied (scheduler) plus media and resource management options such as the CommVault VaultTracker® feature.

Auxiliary copy allows you to schedule, run on-demand, save a job as a script, or set an automatic copy. When configuring Auxiliary copy operations there are several options you can configure:

- Allocate number of drives to use during auxiliary copy
- Which secondary copies you want to include in the auxiliary copy
- Start new media and mark media full which can be used to isolate jobs on media
- Vault tracker options which can be used to export and track media using VaultTracker™ policies and reports
- Job priorities to assign different job priorities for auxiliary copies

Allocating Resources for Auxiliary Copies

When running auxiliary copies it is important to determine how many drives you want to use. By default an auxiliary copy operation will use one drive. The option to specify drives is the *Number of Streams to Copy in Parallel*.

When you configure an auxiliary copy you can specify which storage policy secondary copies you want to associate with the operation. You can also specify how many streams the secondary copy will use with the combine to streams option. Depending on how many copies and the combine to streams number, you may need to allocate more drives to ensure the auxiliary copies get done within their specified windows.

Example: You schedule an auxiliary copy with two secondary copies. You use the default setting for number of streams to copy in parallel which is 1. What results is that 1 tape is loaded in 1 drive and the first stream is copied. Then the tape is unloaded and a new one is inserted to copy the second stream. This can result in the auxiliary copies taking too long and they may underutilize the library.

Solution: Set the number of streams to copy in parallel to 2. Now the auxiliary copy will load 2 tapes in 2 drives and both copies will be run simultaneously.

Figure 3-8: *Allocating two drives for auxiliary copy operations by setting the number of streams to copy in parallel to two.*

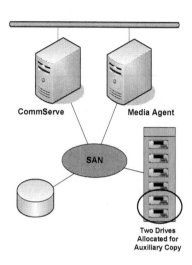

Two Drives
Allocated for
Auxiliary Copy

It is important to understand why CommVault software will only allocate 1 drive by default. A tape library may be used for auxiliary copies and also production backups at the same time. You wouldn't want to allocate every drive in a library to auxiliary copies if you need some of those drives for backups as well.

You have to tell the software how many drives you want to use. It will never assume that if there are six drives available that it will use all of them. Allocate the number of drives so you can meet your backup requirements. Plan this out carefully to reduce the amount of media movements within the library.

Automatic Copy

Most jobs run once during a day and a normal schedule can be used for auxiliary copies. The automatic copy feature allows you set a check interval for source data to be copied. This can be a great advantage when jobs are being run multiple times per day or if you are unsure when the source data will be available for copy.

Example: A critical database is running transaction log backups every four hours. You want to run an auxiliary copy of the source transaction logs to a secondary location, in this case a magnetic library off-site.

Solution: Schedule the transaction logs to backup every four hours. Then set the automatic copy option to check for source data. If source data is present the auxiliary copy will run creating an additional copy of the data.

Data Path for Auxiliary Copies

When configuring primary backups you define the path data will take to its destination. You can also use GridStor technology to define multiple paths to provide LAN-Free paths, load balancing, or failover. Auxiliary copies work a little different than that.

The idea of using CommVault storage policies is to manage data within a backup environment with as little impact to your production environment. Because of this, an auxiliary copy will always attempt a LAN-Free backup. If a LAN-Free path is not available it will use the default path. You can add data paths to the secondary copy to provide LAN-Free paths when possible.

Example: Production server backs up through Media Agent 1 to a magnetic library in a SAN. Media Agent 2 is zoned to see the magnetic library and a tape library. Media Agent 1 is only zoned to see the magnetic library. You want to use a LAN-Free path to move the data from the magnetic library to the tape library.

Solution: In the secondary copy of the storage policy which will move the data from the magnetic library to the tape library, add the data path of Media Agent 2 and the tape library. When backups are performed Media Agent 1 will backup data to the magnetic library. When the auxiliary copy is performed Media Agent 2 will copy the data from the magnetic library to the tape library.

Figure 3-9: Production backups use Media Agent 1. Auxiliary copy operations use Media Agent 2 to perform LAN-Free backup to a tape library.

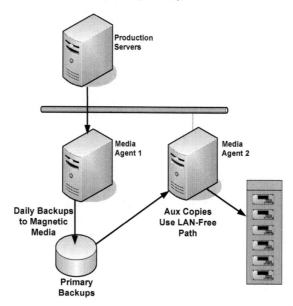

Chapter 4

Defining Retention for Data Lifecycle Management

Chapter Summary
- Evolution of storage management needs
- Business requirements driving retention
- Business and government regulations driving retention
- Rules for configuring retention

In order to understand how and why CommVault defines retention the way they do, a little history must be discussed. Traditionally data was backed up directly to tape and brought off-site for safe keeping. In those days, when computers were still a new idea, electronic data was a secondary source of information. Most information was still maintained through paper record keeping. If electronic data was lost, it could be recreated, though sometimes at a high cost, by the company.

As the amount of electronic data began to grow it became apparent that simple backups would not be enough. The first change was to perform full backups of all data during the weekend when computer systems were not being used. Then during the week smaller backups would be performed. Incremental backups of data that was changed from the previous nights backup or differential backups of data changed since the last full would be used to ensure all data was protected. The full and the incrementals or differentials became known as a cycle.

Figure 4-1: Using Fulls, Incrementals, and differentials to define cycles

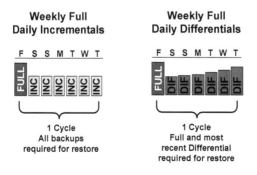

As electronic data began to replace paper record keeping, it became important to maintain multiple copies of electronic data. Bringing one tape to an off-site location would not provide any protection if the tape was lost, damaged or the location burned down. Multiple copies would have to be created. Now data was being kept on and off site. Recent backups would be kept on-site and older backups would be moved off-site. Concepts such as keeping weekly fulls on-site, monthly fulls off-site, and quarterly or yearly fulls off-site for long term archiving became the common method for protecting data. This became known as Grandfather, Father, Son methods. More importantly the concept of tape rotation schemes became standard practice for businesses.

Figure 4-2: *Tape rotation scheme for daily incrementals, weekly fulls, monthly fulls and yearly fulls*

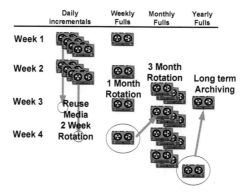

One of the most common questions I get asked is "Why does CommVault® software define retention the way they do?" The simple answer I give is "Options!" no matter what type of media rotation scheme you want, no matter how you want to manage logical data, CommVault software can meet your needs. From simple 3 week rotations to complex rotations based on data type and physical location, CommVault software gives you the flexibility. One of the key features of this product is the ability to define your business needs and then implement strategies to meet those needs. You should never have to say at any business meeting "We can't do it that way, the software won't let us."

Key Requirements in Determining Retention

When defining retention within a storage policy there is one critical statement that must be made:

Retention settings should be based on business needs to protect data.

This is the primary decision driving retention configurations. Retention decisions should not be made solely by backup administrators. Meetings with all key decision makers, auditors, and any outside consultants should be conducted. All needs should be addressed and retention should be based on the results of these meetings.

In a perfect world all data would be kept forever, but in the real world this is not always possible. A key element to remember is the advantage of logically addressing data within an environment. This allows businesses to determine retention strategies based on business systems rather than physical servers.

Example: A database server has several databases with a total of 2 Terabytes of information. Backing up this server and retaining the data for 5 years may be impractical. Through business meetings it is determined that a key database holding financial information must be backed up weekly and retained for 5 years. The database is 4 Gigabytes in size.

Solution: Define a subclient pointing to the database. Then the database can be logically managed independently from the rest of the data on the server. Retaining 4 GB of data for 5 years is much more practical then retaining 2 TB.

There are several key issues that must be discussed when planning a retention strategy:

1. Business and government regulations
2. Business reputation & customer confidence
3. Current capacity and planned growth
4. Budgetary limitations
5. Risk assessment

Business and Government Regulations

Regulations such as Sarbanes-Oxley, HIPAA, and Gramm-Leach-Bliley have forced industry to look closer at how they protect information. This can be a difficult task, especially when there are no clear cut rules for retaining information. I have seen many businesses that infinitely retain critical data such as e-mail and financial records. They have no choice since government regulations provide guidelines that can be interpreted differently depending on which auditor you ask.

In explaining retention to a customer they asked "How long should we retain data for?" My response was "As long as your company tells you to!" Of course their response was "They don't know!" The problem they had was there was no top driven data retention policy within the company and retention decisions were being made by the IT staff based on storage space and budget. This is definitely the wrong way to approach retention. Business and government requirements will most likely be the most critical variable in determining data retention needs.

Business Reputation and Customer Confidence

Depending on the type of business, reputation and customer confidence could be a huge determining factor in setting retention requirements. If you used a free E-mail service and one day you logged on to find only one message in your inbox you would probably be concerned. On opening that e-mail you realize that it is an apology letter that all mail had been lost and they are sorry. Would you continue to use their service?

I like to qualify disasters as sympathetic and non-sympathetic. Disasters such as Katrina, the 2003 Northeast power outage, and 9/11 all qualify as sympathetic disasters. Customers are more likely to understand the situation and accept data loss or interruption in service. On the other hand, if your building catches fire and burns to the ground, and you never properly protected data or maintained off-site copies, then customers may not be as sympathetic because you were not proactive in being prepared for such an event.

In both cases, determine your customer base and user base and consider how data loss may affect your ability to continue to do business and retain customers.

Current Capacity and Planned Growth

You can only retain information based on the capacity to hold the data. Analyzing your current ability to store information will give you a starting point for determining retention capability. If capability does not meet requirement you'll need to purchase more storage. Considerations must be paid to expected data growth. This includes the following determining factors:

- Incremental rate of change for existing data
- Projected trends based on historical data
- New projects which may implement new business systems
- Number of copies of protected data and locations for the copies

You need to consider how much data and where it will be stored. Historical information could be placed on tape to be archived off-site. User data may be required to be kept on fast disks for easy recovery. Capacity must be thought not as a total but broken down based on location of media, ease of access, and speed of recovery. Do not underestimate the amount of protected data that will need to be managed or you may find yourself running out of space.

Budgetary Limitations

Determining retention requirements may force a company to invest in more equipment to accomplish retention goals. However, budgetary limitations can affect the overall retention strategy and force you to readdress retention issues. Legacy hardware that has not reached the end of its lifecycle and strict budgets may force you to make due with what you have. This may ultimately effect retention settings and force you to readdress retention strategies.

Risk Assessment

There are many different definitions of a disaster. For smaller companies, losing even one server can be catastrophic. Larger companies that cluster servers and store data on RAID arrays may think on a broader scale and consider a building loss as a disaster. Companies implementing site replication technologies could possibly sustain a site loss but with a larger cost of implementing and maintaining this type of storage infrastructure.

Placing data off-site for most companies is essential. Where to locate off-site data is a key issue. I was working for a company in southern California and after several meetings I convinced them to store data off-site. The office manager would take a tape home each night. The problem was that she lived five minutes from the building. I explained that with the potential for earthquakes, storing our backup data several miles from the office was unacceptable. Then I asked them what they would do if they lost all their data. Their response was "We work in a closely tied industry where we know everyone personally that we do business with. We would simply call them and reconstruct the information that was lost." Their risk assessment was low since information could be recreated if lost. So they kept the data several minutes from the office.

Several years later I was talking to someone from the company. They told me they implemented a new database system using replication and implemented a very detailed disaster recovery strategy. I asked him what changed their mind and he responded "Sarbanes-Oxley!"

What to Discuss at the Meeting

Any meetings discussing data storage and retention should be focused on two key goals: Define data storage requirements for business regulations, and define disaster recovery and business continuity strategies.

Key points to bring up during meetings:

- Current strategies for dealing with retention.
- Guidelines imposed by business and government regulations.
- Perceived risk of disaster.
- *Recovery Time Objectives* and *Recovery Point Objectives* for critical business systems.
- Time and resources required to properly document and test DR procedures.

The following is a list of general guidelines that gives you a starting point. However, and I stress this strongly, these points are just general guidelines.

- Key decision makers all the way up the ladder need to be involved in determining information retention.
- Talk with all system administrators and listen to their needs. Harvest their expertise since they should know their systems better then you.
- Consider external consultants because they will have the expertise and will not be bias based on status quo or what I like to call "legacy issues" within a company.
- Document all retention strategies and have key decision makers sign into effect these policies.
- At no point should data retention decisions be left to backup administrators.

Chapter 8 will discuss methods for approaching protection and retention strategies in more detail.

Understanding Retention for Standard Backup iDataAgents

The following section focuses on step-by-step explanations on how retention works within CommVault software. By understanding the logic and rules of retention, a thorough understanding will be gained allowing you to configure retention to meet all business and media management requirements.

Retention Rules

The methodology CommVault software uses in defining retention is confusing to many people. Understanding why it is defined this way will help to clarify retention and allow you to configure it correctly.

First part of understanding retention for backup data is to know the rules:

1. Retention for backup data is defined in CYCLES and DAYS.
2. Both CYCLES and DAYS criteria must be met before data will age.
3. Data is aged in complete cycles. Fulls and any dependent jobs (incrementals/differentials) associated with the full will be aged together.
4. Cycles are variables depending on when a full is run and completed successfully.
5. Days are constants based on a 24 hour time period.
6. The data aging process checks protected jobs against the retention configured within the storage policy copy. Any jobs which meet retention criteria will be aged and depending on CommVault configurations may also be pruned.

Let's take a closer look at these rules by using some examples. Not all of these examples will make real world sense but they are used to prove each rule.

Rule 1: Retention for Backup Data is defined in DAYS and CYCLES
Retention is notated as (*Cycles, Days*). So (2, 14) represents 2 cycles and 14 days.

Cycles
In the retention tab of the storage policy copy, retention can be defined for standard agent types and archive agents. Note that the cycle criteria is not available for archive retention. This is due to the nature of standard backup data. Backup data is used for disaster recovery, data recovery, as well as long term archiving of backup data. For all backup data, it is essential to maintain complete backup sets. A complete set will include a full, all incrementals, or differentials. This set represents all data on the system required for recovery in the event of data loss.

Many people think that a cycle is a week long or that a cycle isn't really a cycle unless the full and all scheduled incrementals/differentials have been completed. This is not necessarily true. The true definition of a cycle is a complete set of backups required to recover a system to the state of the most recent backup.

Example: A typical backup strategy of weekly fulls and daily incrementals is being performed.

Figure 4-3: A typical weekly cycle with a full and six incremental backup operations.

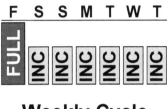

Weekly Cycle

This does represent a cycle but what if the following week you perform a full backup on Friday an incremental on Saturday and the server crashes on Sunday. The full and the incremental represent all data on that system required for restore. This means that it is technically a cycle.

Figure 4-4: Illustration depicting a system crash mid cycle. This is why CommVault software will use Cycles and Days in defining retention.

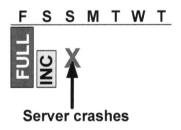

It is important to make a distinction between the two concepts regarding cycles. What is a cycle and what is a complete cycle. A cycle is a full data protection operation. As soon as the full completes successfully it is a cycle. Once that full finishes successfully it also marks the previous cycle as complete. This is important to know since cycles will age off based on the number of complete cycles.

Example: There are 8 days of backups. The first week containing a full and six incrementals and the second week with one full. There are two cycles, one is complete and the other has just started but is considered a cycle based on the idea that it represents all data required to recover a system to the state of the most recent backup.

Figure 4-5: two cycles have been performed. The first is a complete cycle but the second, though not complete does contain all data required to recover a system to the most recent backup point.

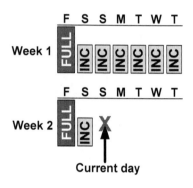

Days
A day represents a 24 hour time period. This period is counted from the time that a data protection operation completes.

Rule 2: Both CYCLES and DAYS criteria must be met before Data will age

CommVault uses AND logic to ensure that both retention parameters configured are satisfied. Another way of looking at this would be that the longest retention setting within a storage policy copy will always determine the time data will be retained for.

Example: Retention for a storage policy copy is set to (2, 3) or 2 cycles and 3 days. Now this example doesn't make sense in the real world but it is being used to prove out the statement that both days and cycles criteria must be met for data to age.

Figure 4-6: Retention set to 2 cycles and 3 days performing full backups daily. Cycles criteria has been met but not Days criteria.

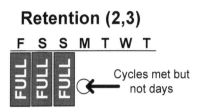

Retention (2,3)

On Monday three fulls have been performed. If we were to age Friday's full there would be 2 fulls left meeting our criteria of 2 cycles. However, the days criteria calls for 3 days which would not be met. Another day must be counted before the Friday full will age.

Figure 4-7: Retention criteria of both Cycles and Days has been met and the first full backup will be marked as aged.

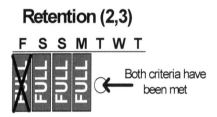

Retention (2,3)

Rule 3: Data is aged in complete cycles

Backup data is managed within a storage policy as a cycle or a set of backups. This will include the full which designates the beginning of a cycle and all incrementals or differentials. When data aging is performed and retention criteria allow for data to be aged, the entire cycle is marked as aged. This process ensures that jobs will not become orphaned resulting in dependant jobs (incremental or differential) existing without the associated full.

Example: This is another far fetched retention example used to prove out the rule. Retention is configured for (2, 7) 2 cycles and 7 days. Fulls are being performed on Fridays and Mondays, and incrementals on all other days. On Saturday the cycles criteria of 2 has been met meaning that if I removed a cycle there would be 2 left, a complete cycle (Monday – Thursday) and the full on Friday night. However, since we prune entire cycles we would have to age the Friday full and the incrementals from Saturday and Sunday. This would result in only 5 days which does not meet our days retention requirements of 7. So on Monday when the data aging operation runs (default 12PM daily) there will now be 2 cycles and 7 days which will allow the first cycle to be aged.

Figure 4-8: Retention has been defined for 2 Cycles and 7 Days. Cycles criteria has been met but not the days criteria.

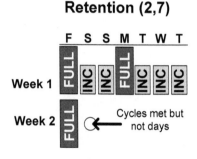

Figure 4-9: Retention has been defined for 2 Cycles and 7 Days. On Monday both cycles and days criteria have been met and the first cycle will be marked as aged.

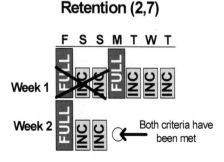

Rule 4: Cycles are variables based on a successful completion of a Full backup

CommVault software defines the start of a cycle based on the successful completion of a full backup. A successful full is essential to ensure that all data required to recover a business system is available. If a full does not complete successfully a cycle will continue. If a full is manually run mid cycle a new cycle will start. This is why a cycle is considered a variable.

Example 1: Weekly fulls and daily incrementals are being performed. A Friday full did not complete successfully resulting in the cycle to continue resulting in a 14 day cycle.

Figure 4-10: Failure of a full backup results in a cycle continuing until a valid full data protection operation is performed.

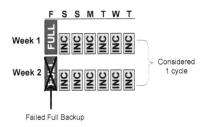

Example 2: Due to compliance a full backup is being performed on the last day of the quarter which is on a Monday. Normally scheduled full operations run on a Friday. Although the Monday night full is not part of the normal schedule it still results in the start of a new cycle.

Figure 4-11: A full backup is performed on the last day of the quarter effecting the cycle criteria of a subclient.

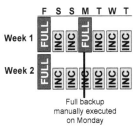

Rule 5: Days are Constants Based on 24 Hour Time Period

A day will be measured as a 24 hour time period from the completion time of a data protection operation. Days are considered constants since regardless of a backup being performed or completed successfully the time period will always be counted. If a backup fails, backups are not scheduled or if power goes out a day will still count towards retention. This is why it is so critical to measure retention in cycles and days. If retention was just managed by days and no backups were run for a few weeks all backup data may age off leaving no backups.

Example: During a Friday night backup power is lost in the building. Power is restored on Sunday resulting in two days elapsing and counting towards retention. Note that since the Friday full failed the cycle continues into the next scheduled full (following Friday). This illustrates the importance of defining retention in both cycles and days.

Figure 4-12: A failure of a full backup on Friday due to a power outage results in a cycle continuing until a valid full is completed.

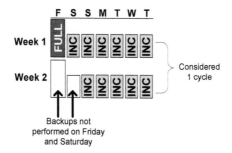

Interesting note:
The default retention for a storage policy copy is infinite which is set by a check box. After deselecting the check box the default retention is 2 cycles and 15 days. The 15th day results in another full being performed before aging will occur for the first cycle. Now although this may be thought of as a good thing that the extra full is performed, what if the full fails to complete? In this case it is the 15 days setting that is forcing data to be retained here, not the cycles. The result of a failed full backup will have no effect on the aging of the first cycle in the diagram.

http://www.commvault.com/training

Figure 4-13: *Retention configured to 2 cycles and 15 days results in another full being performed. The fact that the cycles criteria is set to 2 does not guarantee that the full must be completed successfully.*

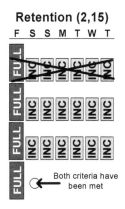

The key point here is this: If you want to retain 3 cycles of data, set the cycles to 3. Don't try to figure out how many days there are in 3 cycles as it will not guarantee the protection you need. On the other hand if you need 2 cycles on hand at any given time changing the 15 to a 14 could potentially save quite a bit of media since the first cycle will age on Friday at 12 PM before the Friday full is performed. This will free up media to run that Friday full.

Figure 4-14: *Setting retention to 2 cycles and 14 days results in the first cycles being aged on the Friday.*

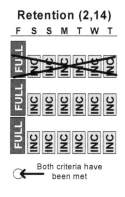

Rule 6: Data will be aged based on retention criteria

Data aging is the process in which data in protected storage is compared with the settings of the storage policy copy. Both cycles and days are compared to the backup job. Any data that has exceeded retention will become aged. Depending on certain environment conditions the data may also be pruned or deleted.

The following chart explains conditions which may or may not result in data being pruned from media.

Media	Data Aging Results
Tape Media	Data will be marked as aged but not pruned. Once all jobs on tape media have been marked aged the tape will be placed back in the default scratch pool and overwritten with new backup data.
Magnetic Media	By default when a job is marked aged it will be pruned from magnetic media. A storage policy option to Use Managed Disk Space can be enabled. This will effectively retain the data on media beyond the retention period. Data will be pruned from media based on thresholds set in the magnetic library configuration options.

Why Cycles and Days?

The method CommVault software uses to define retention can be confusing. The first part of defining retention is at the meetings with the decision makers. Once that is settled it is time to implement policy. Consider the three reasons why data is protected.

1. Disaster recovery
2. Data recovery
3. Data archiving

Disaster Recovery

When considering disaster recovery retention the key is determining how many complete sets of data is required to meet retention goals. This means the cycle criteria should be the key configuration. Industry minimum standard for retention for DR is 2 cycles. CommVault has a minimum recommendation of 2 copies of 2 cycles, one copy for on-site and one for off-site.

Data Recovery and Backup Data Archiving

When managing data for long term storage, days should be the determining criteria. If you want to give users the ability to recover home folder data for a period of 90 days, then the days retention should be set to 90. If you want to archive data off-site for a period of 7 years the days retention should be set to 2555 (give or take a day for leap years).

NOTE: The term archiving being used here refers to archiving of backup data. CommVault also has data archiving agents. The method used to handle data is different for archiving agents and is discussed in detail in the Information Lifecycle Management chapter.

Extended Retention

Standard retention allows you to define the length of time based on cycles and days that you want to retain data. Extended retention allows you to define specific retention in days that you want to keep full backups for. It allows you to extend the basic retention by assigning specific retention to fulls based on criteria configured in the extended retention settings. Basically it allows you to set a grandfather, father, son tape rotation scheme.

Example: You want to retain backups for 4 cycles and 28 days. You also want to retain a monthly full for three months, a quarterly full for a year, and a yearly full infinitely.

To accomplish this you configure retention as follows:

- Standard retention is set for (4,28)
- Extended retention is configured for:
    - For 90 days keep monthly fulls
    - For 365 days keep quarterly fulls
    - For infinite keep yearly full

Media Capacity Planning for Retention Goals

In order to meet retention goals there must be enough available media to hold protected data. The first thing to consider is that since CommVault retains and ages data based on full cycles the amount of media available must exceed the amount of data and the length you want to hold it.

Example: If you want to retain data for 2 cycles and 14 days there must be enough media to retain three cycles. The reason is that the third cycle must complete successfully before the first cycle will age.

Figure 4-15: Media capacity planning to keep 2 weeks (cycles) of data on hand requires 3 weeks of storage space. The 3rd cycle must complete before the first cycle will age.

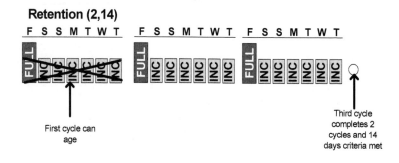

Chapter 5

Information Lifecycle Management

Chapter Summary

- ILM concepts
- Data archiving
- Service Level Agreements
- Data classification
- Using storage policies with ILM

Information Lifecycle Management is an emerging concept which allows organizations to intelligently manage information throughout its useful lifecycle. CommVault® software is one of the leading technologies to allow for the intelligent management of data by logically addressing business data based on the importance of the information to the business and the expected lifecycle of the data.

The term data lifecycle management has been used throughout this book when discussing storage policies and data protection. This term is used because data being grouped into subclients can be managed independently within a backup environment. Information lifecycle management however focuses more specifically on the type of data that is being managed rather then what folders the data exists in.

ILM Concepts

Traditionally files created by a user were small documents that would not take up much space on storage. As the capabilities of applications and the power of computers increased, users would create more elaborate documents embedding pictures, diagrams, and even media files into a document. Over time these files sitting in home folders became difficult to manage and backup times increased.

"Manual ILM", as I like to call it, is the idea of forcing users to clean out old files they no longer need. Problems came about since many people would not delete files, and those who did would often ask for them to be recovered later on because "It's very important and I need it back now!"

Information Lifecycle Management automates the archiving of older data through the use of policies. These policies are determined by business needs. As files become older they are moved or *archived* to less expensive media. Archived files can still be accessible to the user either through stub files which point to the actual data, by conducting index searches, or both.

Figure 5-1: *ILM tiered storage management*

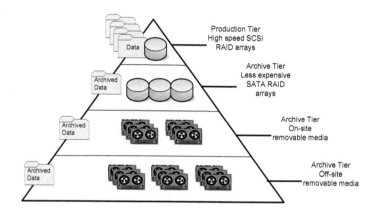

Data Archiver

Archiving data is the process of moving information to less expensive secondary storage. This shrinks the size of primary storage which results in less space required to hold the data and smaller backup windows when protecting the data. Data Archiving is also referred to as *Hierarchal Storage Management* or HSM.

Archived data can still be retrieved through the use of stub files. Stub files contain information pointing to the location of the original file. Depending on the OS or application being used, stub files may work differently but the general concept will be the same. When a user wants a file they open the stub file which initiates a recovery of the original file from secondary storage.

Stub files are not the only way to recover archived data. Files can be content indexed and users can search for files based on what they remember in the contents of the file itself.

Example: A user is looking for a word document that is several years old. There is a specific section they want to use in a new document. The user does not remember the name of the file so they perform a content search. He does remember content from the file so they use what they remember as the basis of the search. Search results return the correct file, they recall it, and extract the information they need to create the new document.

In version 6.1 of CommVault software the term archiving was defined differently. The concept of data archiving being discussed in this chapter was called *Data Migrator* in the 6.1 version. To make things more confusing there was also a *Data Archiver* in 6.1. This referred to the archiving of Exchange E-mail through the use of the Exchange journaling feature. In 7.0 the terms we now use are:

- **Data Archiver** which removes data from the source location to secondary storage
- **Compliance Archiver** which can be used with the Exchange Journal feature

Service Level Agreement

As data becomes older the chances of it being needed diminishes. A *Service Level Agreement* or SLA can be defined stating that the older the data is the longer it will take to recover the information. Traditional data archiving would define policies to archive all data within specified folders. The idea of ILM is to set SLA's for different data owned by different people within an organization.

Example: The engineering department in a company generates large CAD files containing schematics for various projects. Once the projects are over the CAD files must be kept for legal reasons. 5 years later if something goes wrong with the project, engineers must have the ability to go back to old diagrams to find out what went wrong. Through business meetings with the engineering department it is determined that the probability of CAD files being accessed drops after 3 years. However, there have been emergency cases within a period of 6 years that CAD files had to be accessed. All CAD files must be kept forever.

Meetings with the finance group were also conducted to determine SLA's for finance records. Spreadsheets are frequently accessed within the fiscal year. Once the year closes the files still may need to be accessed for the next year. Beyond that time it is unlikely the files will be needed, but again they must be kept forever.

Based on meetings the following chart illustrates the SLA for CAD and XLS files.

		Service Level Agreement			
Group	File types	Tier 1 – instant	Tier 2- near instant	Tier 3- 24 hours	Tier 4- 2 days
Engineering	CAD	3 years	3 years	4 years	Infinite
Finance	XLS	2 years	3 years	5 years	infinite

Data Classification

CommVault software implements ILM through the use of *Data Classification*. Data classification works by monitoring Windows Change Journal and generating a database that represents all data within the drive being monitored. Information such as the file name, extension, modification, and owner is kept in this database. When archiving jobs are performed using data classification, the database is queried allowing data to be managed based on ILM needs.

Using data classification, businesses can define elaborate ILM structures which can greatly improve data management. Data Classification can easily be implemented into current CommCell® environments by deploying licenses to file servers which will be using the features. All configurations are done in the CommCell console using familiar subclients, storage policies, and retention.

Storage Policies and ILM

What is represented as a triangle in the ILM diagram is represented in a storage policy as a cloud. So the concept of ILM easily integrates with CommVault storage policies. The only modules that need to be added is the appropriate archiving agent and the Data *Classification Enabler* or DCE agent.

Figure 5-2: *Sample ILM diagram (left) and storage policy configuration to meet SLA goals (right)*

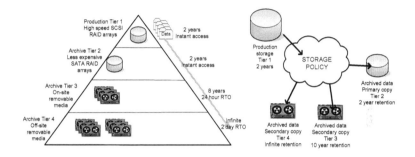

Using ILM concepts and CommVault storage policies, elaborate SLA designs can be implemented. Multiple copies within each policy can be created representing different SLA's for business data. Data classification can be used to define data based on what types of files and who owns the data.

Since storage policies create multiple copies of data, as the information ages the time to recover (SLA) will increase. Recovering from disk will always be fast for the user. Data can also be copied to tape. This actually serves two purposes. Moving data to tape for long term archiving will free up space on disk storage. Creating multiple copies to tape also allows the data to be kept in secure on-site and off-site locations providing disaster recovery in the event of disk loss or site loss.

Figure 5-3: Complex storage policy designs allowing for flexible ILM definitions with different SLA's for business data.

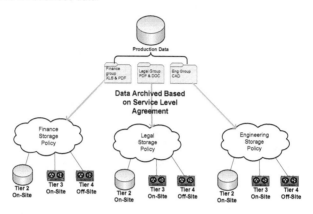

ILM, Data Classification, and Content Indexing

One of the biggest evolutionary changes to CommVault Simpana® software is the ease of integration of Data Classification and *Content Indexing* when defining an ILM strategy. As data gets older and its usefulness decreases the data is moved to secondary storage. After a time, files become forgotten and just take up space. People come and go within your company; great ideas are created and then sometimes forgotten. The ability to perform data mining or knowledge discovery can be a huge asset to a company.

Example: Several employees in your research and development department are working on a new project. Someone informs them that they remember a similar idea that was being worked out several years ago. All of the work performed was by employees no longer with the company and all the data is now lost and forgotten.

Solution: By archiving and content indexing data, the employees can actually mine archived data. This will hopefully allow them to get a head start on their project and not have to repeat work already done. Content searches can be performed based on permissions in Active Directory. In this case the research and development group can mine all files that the group owns. In this example, the results are several key documents already created providing them a wealth of information on the project they are currently working on.

Advantages of ILM and CommVault® Software

The ease of integration with your existing CommCell environment makes ILM a strong solution for dealing with large amounts of information.

Benefits of implementing ILM with CommVault Technologies

- Shorter backup times
- More efficient use of production storage
- Intelligent management of business data
- Policy driven archiving
- Reduce media usage in backup environment
- Allow longer retention of data

With increasing requirements for data storage and the increasing size of data being stored, intelligent management of data is becoming a crucial aspect of data protection. Implementing ILM strategies with data classification and content indexing can meet business needs and establish a foundation in which data can be protected and archived within your organization for years to come.

CommVault strongly recommends consulting with Professional Services before attempting to implement strategies such as content indexing.

Chapter 6

Advanced CommVault® Concepts

Chapter Summary
- Data path override
- Managed disk space
- GridStor™ technologies for failover, load balancing, and LAN-free backups
- Data path override
- Single Instance Storage
- Synthetic full backups
- Incremental storage policies
- Considerations for database backups
- Restore by job
- Custom business calendars

The following chapter will deal with advanced CommVault® features. Depending on licensing arrangements these features may or may not be available. Some of these features do not tie in directly with storage policies but they will be used in Part II of this book where we will focus on different solutions which can be implemented using CommVault features.

IMPORTANT

This section is designed to provide a general conceptual overview of CommVault features. It is not intended to provide in-depth descriptions or configuration options for these features. Refer to CommVault's Online Documentation for more information, and also consider the Common Technology Engine quick reference book by M.C. Dahlmeier.

Data Path Override

One of the objectives when defining CommVault storage policies is to limit the number of policies used. This can become more complex when you have multiple Media Agents writing to different libraries.

Example: You want to backup several servers over the production network and load balance them through two Media Agents. You also have a Database server you want to perform LAN free backups for. For off-site disaster recovery you want to consolidate all three servers to one tape.

Figure 6-1: 2 media agents are dedicated for LAN backups and a 3rd media agent dedicated for LAN-Free backups of a SAN attached server.

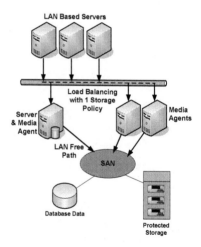

Solution 1: If you create a single storage policy and configure three data paths for all three Media Agents, the database server will perform LAN free backups. However there would be the potential of LAN based backups using the Media Agent on the database server to load balance backups. Although the single storage policy will allow you to consolidate the three servers to one tape, the resulting load balancing using the database Media Agent could have negative effects on the database server.

Solution 2: Create a single storage policy defining all three paths for load balancing. The database server will always use the LAN free path. In each subclient of the LAN backup servers configure data path override not to use the database Media Agent. Now they will only load balance between the two dedicated Media Agents.

Figure 6-2: All subclients on LAN servers are configured to only use dedicated media agents by specifying the paths in the data path override configuration.

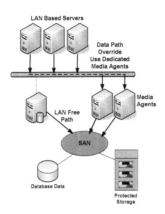

Managed Disk Space

Managed Disk Space is a feature used with magnetic libraries which allows data to reside on the disk beyond its retention settings. This allows you to increase the chances of recovering data faster from primary storage on disk without changing retention settings. Managed data on disk is treated the same as retained data for data recovery.

Managed data will be held on the disk beyond the standard retention settings until an upper threshold is reached. A monitoring process will detect data exceeding the upper threshold and then delete aged jobs from the media until a lower threshold is reached. It is important to note that only aged jobs will be pruned. If all aged jobs are pruned and the lower threshold is not met no more pruning will occur.

Managed disk thresholds are configured in the magnetic library properties and can be enabled in each storage policy copy.

As a general rule of thumb the upper threshold should be set to allow one hour of backups to run after the threshold is reached. The lower threshold should be set so that the managed disk space pruning operation will not run more then once in a backup time period as the pruning operation will have a negative effect on the performance of backups. For more information on configuring library settings for managed disk space see CommVault's online documentation.

Example: User data on a file server has a recovery window for a period of 90 days. Magnetic media can hold up to two months of data. To increase the potential of being able to recover data from magnetic media and not have to recall tapes, the managed disk space option will be used.

Solution: Create two storage policies. The first will write data to disk for a standard (2,14) retention. The second policy will also have a (2,14) retention but managed disk space will be enabled. All DR data will be directed to the first storage policy. After the (2,14) retention is exceeded the data will be pruned. User data will point to the second policy. User data will remain on the disk until the upper threshold is reached at which point jobs will be pruned. A secondary copy to tape will be created with a retention of (12,90) to ensure that user data is being protected for the full 90 days.

Figure 6-3: Diagram illustrating the use of two storage policies to backup one file server. Managed disk space is only enabled on the second policy where user data is being managed. This increases the chances of recovering user data from disk.

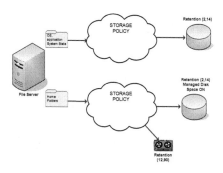

Spool Copy

The *Spool Copy* option can be used to take advantage of fast disk read/write access and its multistreaming capabilities when there is limited capacity available on the disks. A spool copy is a no retention copy. Data is spooled to disk and then copied to a secondary copy. Once the data is successfully copied to the secondary copy, the data on disk will be pruned.

Single Instance Storage

Consider a DLL file being backed up on a Windows server. Each week this file will be backed up during a full data protection operation. Now consider 50 Windows servers all backing up that same DLL file. Each weekly full of each server will back up that same DLL file over and over again. Over time there may be 100's of copies of that same file in storage. Single Instance Storage can reduce those 100's of copies down to 1 providing greatly improved storage capacity.

Single Instancing works with magnetic disk libraries. A database called the SIDB maintains a table of all files. If a file being written to disk is the same as a file already in storage, the new file being written to disk will be deleted.

Single Instancing is also referred to as *Data De-Duplication*. There is an important distinction to be made regarding methods of data de-duplication. Dedicated hardware can be used to perform data de-duplication. This dedicated hardware can be used with CommVault software but all de-duplication processes are external to CommVault. These dedicated hardware solutions perform data de-duplication at the block level. This is good for file backups as well as database backups.

CommVault software's de-duplication process will single instance file data. In other words the de-duplication is performed at the file level. This works well with file system data and object level backups (such as SharePoint documents or E-mail) but does not work well with database backups.

The main advantages of CommVault single instancing is that it does not require dedicated hardware as it will work on any disk storage and it is also simple to deploy and use in an existing CommVault environment.

Synthetic Full Backups

Full backups can require a lot of bandwidth to complete. Backups over high speed LAN or SAN based backups can handle large amounts of data traffic. Slower LAN or WAN based backups can create bottleneck and even saturate the network limiting other communications. *Synthetic full* backups synthesize backups by consolidating data from previous backups into a new full backup.

Each day when an incremental is performed all data within the backup environment is the same that exists in the production environment. A synthetic full will grab that data from the previous full and any incrementals created after the full and write them into a new full backup. This full will become the basis of the new cycle and will be treated as a normal full by CommVault retention settings.

Figure 6-4: *Synthetic full generated from previous cycle. All files that existed when the latest image was taken will be copied over to the new Synthetic Full.*

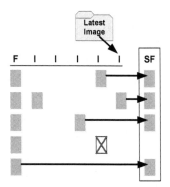

Incremental Storage Policies

Traditionally backup data would all go to one location. All fulls, incrementals, or differentials would all be backed up to the same media location. With backup windows shrinking and protected data growing, more flexibility is needed to meet business goals.

Incremental storage policies allow the configuration of a storage policy link to connect two policies. One policy will define a data path where full backups will be performed. The other policy will define the path for incrementals or differentials.

Example: At a worldwide organization, a file server works around the clock serving user requests and needs to be backed up. During the week a short operation window has been defined. With a lesser workload on weekends, the operation window is more flexible. You have a magnetic library that you want to use but the amount of space required for the full backups exceeds the capacity of your disk library.

Solution: Create an incremental storage policy. The full storage policy will write to tape over the weekend when operation windows are more flexible. During the week incrementals will be written to disk to meet smaller backup windows.

Figure 6-5: An incremental storage policy is configured so all full backups will go to tape and all incremental backups will go to disk.

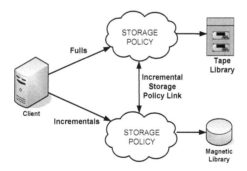

Considerations for Database backups

When CommVault software backs up database application data we will interface with the API's of the application. Some applications offer advanced features allowing CommVault Simpana® software to back them up more efficiently.

Transaction Log Storage Policies

Some database iDataAgents permit you to select a different storage policy for full or differential backups and a different policy for transaction log backups. This is the same concept of incremental storage policies allowing you to send transaction log data to disk and fulls/differentials to tape. This can be especially important when performing frequent transaction log backups during the day when keeping a short recovery point objective.

Considerations for Microsoft SQL, Sybase, and DB2

Databases can become quite large over time. Multistreaming backup jobs can improve the performance when using database application iDataAgents. For the multithreading applications MS-SQL, Sybase, and DB2 multiple streams can greatly improve backup performance. However, due to the nature of these applications when using parallel streams to backup you must also restore with parallel streams. In other words, if you back up 3 streams to 3 tapes, you must have 3 drives available for restore. In addition, MS-SQL, Sybase, and DB2 multi-streamed jobs cannot incorporate features such as multiplexing or combine-to-streams.

Multistreaming a subclient of MS-SQL, Sybase, or DB2 is not the only way to improve the performance of backups. You can also create multiple subclients each using a single stream. Each subclient will represent their own job which means they can be multiplexed or combined to stream. Realize however that in this case the jobs will be restored one at a time.

When creating a secondary copy and setting the Combine to Stream option, a warning box will appear stating that multi-streamed MS-SQL, Sybase, or DB2 jobs will not be copied. The truth is that the job will be copied but you will not be able to restore the data. In order to restore the data, another secondary copy would have to be created with a data path to magnetic disk. You would have to run an Auxiliary copy to the disk to stage the data to be restored to the server. Though this may be a good emergency solution, you should try to avoid this scenario altogether as it will slow down the restore process.

File System Agent or Database Application Agent?

Our database application agents are powerful tools for efficient backups. By interfacing with the application many manual tasks that would be performed by DBAs can instead be automated through the CommCell® console. However many organizations still stick to the old way of dumping databases and using a normal file level backup to protect the data. The negative effect of this is that there will be a two-stage backup and recovery process.

Recommendations are for larger database servers to use a dedicated database iDataAgent to take full advantage of Simpana software and database application features. For smaller databases that can easily be dumped and backed up the file system approach to protecting data is acceptable. Always consider backup windows and the RTO and RPO of the business data.

Restore by Job

Data defined as logical subclients can be managed as independent jobs allowing flexibility in scheduling and the ability to multistream backup jobs. This can improve backup performance but can also have an advantage on restores. Restore by job allows you to select a backup or a series of backups and restore all of them. The two main advantages are that it will be a non-index restore and the restore can be multi-streamed, if multiple streams were used during backup.

Example: Home folders location has been defined as a subclient. Streams have been set to 2 to improve backup performance. The backup job runs and each stream is placed on a different tape. The home folders file server has crashed and you want to restore the home folders to an alternate location.

Solution 1: Browse to the home folders location and select the folder structure to restore. This will generate an index table representing all objects and begin seeking out the data on media. This would be a linear or file-by-file restore and will work based on the index table one tape at a time.

Solution 2: perform a restore by job. Select all jobs making up the cycle including the full and all incrementals or the most recent differential. Restore by job is considered a non-index restore and grabs all chunk data and restores the data to the destination. Since an index table is not generated to represent every object being restored, the job will be faster, and the number of streams used to restore will be the same as the backup. In this case the two tapes will be mounted in two drives and data will be restored in parallel.

Figure 6-6: Restore by job operation restoring data to a client from two tapes simultaneously.

Client　　　　**Media Agent**　　　　**Tape Library**

Custom Business Calendars

When dealing with compliance it is critical to meet requirements for archiving information, especially financial data. Selective copies and extended retention allow you to choose fulls at various time periods. If requirements dictate that a quarterly copy of all financial data must be archived for seven years a selective copy or extended retention can be used. Both by default use a standard calendar based on January 1st to December 31st. Custom business calendars allow you to define custom fiscal calendars which can be used to ensure the correct copies will be retained.

A backup administrator had a special requirement to always take the first Friday full of the month and archive that backup. However due to time and media limitations, they could not create an additional copy, instead they wanted to use extended retention rules. The default rules for extended retention could not accommodate this requirement. The solution had to be designed to ensure the first day of the month always started on a Friday.

The solution was to define a custom calendar in which the first day of the year was the first Friday of January. Then every month would have either 28 or 35 days resulting in the next month always starting on the first Friday of the month.

So for the year 2008 the first day of the custom year would be Friday, January 4th. January would have 28 days making Friday, February 1st the first day on the next month. February would have 35 days making Friday, March 7th the first day of the next month. This may be a complicated solution but it demonstrates the flexibility of CommVault to meet business needs.

CommServe® Disaster Recovery Backups

The CommServe® system maintains a metadata database which contains all configuration information for the entire CommCell environment. It is essential that the metadata is properly protected. Every morning by default at 10:00 AM a DR backup is performed which performs an export and backup of critical information on the CommServe server. The Export Phase will export the metadata database, registry hive, and firewall configuration files to a user defined folder location. The Backup Phase will then backup the exported data through a storage policy to protected media.

The backup phase by default will use a dedicated DR backup storage policy. This will isolate CommServe metadata on its own media. You also have the option to place the DR backups into a regular data protection storage policy.

Chapter 7

Implementing Storage Policies

Chapter Summary
- Storage policy design procedures
- Settings for storage policies and auxiliary copy operations
- Flow chart guides for designing and implementing storage policies

This chapter will focus on storage policy design and implementation strategies using all of the knowledge gained to this point. The first section in this chapter will focus on outlining the steps to designing and creating a storage policy strategy. This will be broken into the following sections:

- Basic approach to policy design
- Determining business requirements
- Determining storage policy designs

Each section will contain a series of descriptions and diagrams illustrating why storage policy strategies should be implemented. Sections will also contain page references to the second part of the book: CommVault® Solutions and Examples which will provide specific examples on how to implement specific strategies.

The second section contains a number of tables explaining all configuration options for storage policies and auxiliary copy operations. The third section will summarize approaches to policy design into a series of flowcharts. Once the concepts are understood the flow charts can be used as guidelines when implementing your storage policy design.

Basic Approach to Policy Design

Simplifying the approach to designing and implementing storage policies will not only make it easier to implement storage policies but also make it easier to manage your backup environment. There are several key rules that you should follow to ensure a manageable and robust storage policy design strategy.

Keep it Simple

There is no need to complicate your environment by implementing needless storage policies. Too many policies will complicate your management of data and require more media since data cannot be combined between different policies. It is not necessary to create a different policy for every file system and application in your environment, unless that's how business needs require policies to be designed.

In keeping it simple, start with one storage policy. Add more policies based on the needs of your organization. These specific needs will be covered in detail later in this chapter.

Meet Business Objectives

Business objectives should be defined by decision makers within your organization. It should also be understood that in some cases meeting business objective may require purchasing or repurposing equipment or licenses. If objectives can not be met and capacity can not be increased to meet needs, then business needs must be readdressed.

Meet Backup Windows

If you are not meeting backup windows then you do not have a well thought out backup environment. The key objective of data protection is to have as little impact to users as possible. To help in meeting backup windows you can upgrade hardware, change backup schedules, or logically design your environment to modify how data is protected. This section will focus on how to improve CommVault architecture to help meet backup windows.

Meet Media Management Requirements

No matter how much storage capacity you have there will always be a limit on how much data you can hold. It is important to understand that limits on capacity will affect data storage and also data placement on media. Consider placing higher priority data on more accessible media and logically group data based on protection and recovery needs. If media management needs can not be met then capacity will have to be added or business needs readdressed.

Meet Restore Objectives

The only reason we backup data is to restore data. Data should be protected based on business requirements. Recovery Time Objectives and Recovery Point Objectives (discussed in chapter 1) should be clearly defined for all business data. Test restores should be performed to ensure that data can be recovered within the designated restore windows.

Storage Policy Design Procedures

The following section will combine all knowledge of CommVault Simpana® software and storage policy design into guidelines for determining and creating storage policies. It is important that you have a good understanding of everything that has been covered in the book to this point.

Determine Business Requirements

Before storage policies can be designed and implemented data should be grouped by business needs. Protection and recovery objectives should be determined for Disaster recovery, data recovery, and data archiving requirements. As discussed in chapter 4, business meetings should be conducted with all key decision makers to determine data retention needs.

Disaster recovery needs should be based on the RTO and RPO numbers discussed in chapter 1. A determination of how many cycles should be kept on-site and off-site for disaster should also be determined. Each critical business system should have distinct disaster recovery requirements even if the business systems are on the same server. DR needs for recovering a server can be different then business systems running on the server since a business system can potentially be recovered out of place to another server.

Data recovery needs should be based on the ability to recover user data within a timely manner. This time period should be based on pre-determined Service Level Agreements (SLA) for business data. There should be an SLA for the maximum time to recover user data when requested, and this will be tied to the appropriate RPO of the data in question.

Data archiving is based on compliance requirements. This is measured by the length of time that data must be kept for historical data keeping as well as the interval in which data should be protected such as monthly or quarterly backups.

Figure 7-1: *Mind map diagram of determining business requirements for data protection:*

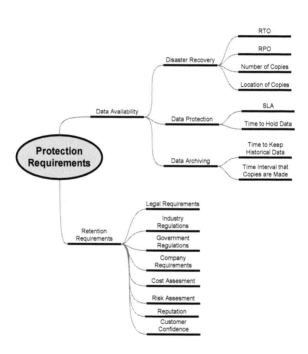

For a thorough look at these requirements refer to Chapter 8 – Storage Policy Case Study.

Determine Storage Policy Designs

To approach policy design, a flow of questions will be presented to determine how many individual policies, copies within a policy, and individual policy settings will be required.

Policy designs Based on Architecture

The physical layout of an environment including number of locations, Media Agent placement, and library locations will play a roll in determining how many policies will be needed. The following questions should be the first determining factors in policy design.

How many locations exist within the CommCell® environment?

The first decision for determining storage policy design will be based on the number of locations where protected data will be backed up to. A CommCell® architecture can be deployed to protect data in many different locations. Data can be centrally backed up over WAN connections to a centralized location or Media Agents can be placed in remote locations to locally protect data within each site.

To determine how many storage policies will be required, you will need to determine how many distinct data paths to protected storage there will be. If each location will have their own media agents and libraries, then each location should have its own storage policies defining distinct data paths to avoid data from being backed up over the WAN. If WAN backups will be performed, storage policies can be consolidated by defining multiple paths within a policy.

Figure 7-2: Storage policy design for multiple locations within a CommCell environment

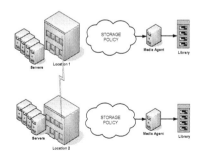

Figure 7-3: WAN Backups from multiple locations using a single storage policy

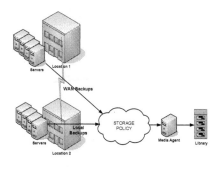

Will there be multiple data paths within a location?

The use of multiple Media Agents or libraries may require multiple storage policies to be defined. If there is only one path being used, then one policy will be needed with regards to data path design. If multiple paths are being used you can use GridStor® technology to define multiple paths within a single policy. If GridStor technology is not being used then each path will require its own storage policy.

Figure 7-4: Multiple storage policies for multiple data paths within a location

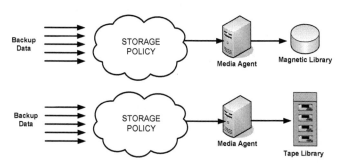

Figure 7-5: Single storage policy defining multiple data paths using GridStor technology

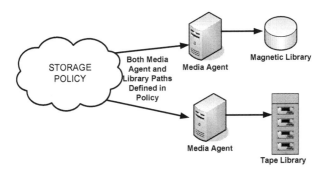

Policy Design Examples	Page
Multiple storage policies using multiple media agents	168
Using GridStor technology to perform LAN-Free backups	210
Using GridStor technology to load balance backups	212
Using GridStor technology for data path failover	214
Consolidating storage policies using data path override	216

Will Different Retention or Locations be required for Primary Backup Data?

In some cases data being backed up to a library may need different storage policies to prevent data from being copied to the same media or to set different retentions for the primary copy. Only one retention setting can be configured for a primary copy. This is to prevent mixed retention types from being copied to the same removable media. If primary copy data requires different retention settings, a policy will be needed for each retention setting.

If primary backup data is going to different media they may also require different storage policies. If data is going to different libraries you can still use one policy by defining multiple data paths and using the data path override option to force subclients to a specific library path.

In some cases you may need to force the division of data even if they are going to the same library. This should not be an issue for magnetic libraries but when using tape libraries and multiplexing, this can be important. You can use different storage policies when using multiplexing to divide business data and prevent data from being multiplexed to the same media.

Additional features such as CommVault sofware's *Single instancing* or *Managed Disk Space* may also require different storage policies to be defined. For single instance storage, CommVault recommends defining specific policies for data that will be single instanced and directing subclient data to those policies. For data that will not be single instanced, direct that data to policies that do not have single instancing enabled. Managed disk space allows data to be retained on disk beyond its basic retention settings. To maximize disk storage and to prevent unwanted data from being retained longer than desired, configure different policies for data that will use managed disk space and data that will not.

Figure 7-6: Multiple storage policies to divide business data and prevent data from being multiplexed to same media

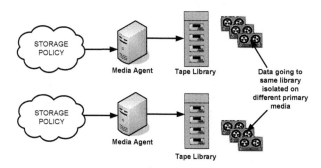

Figure 7-7: Multiple storage policies to define different primary copy retention

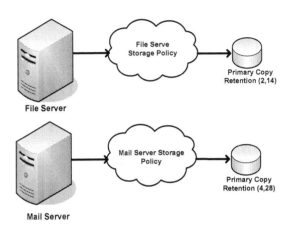

Policy Design Examples	Page
Multiple storage policies to divide business data	164
Multiple storage policies to define different primary retention	166
Consolidating storage policies using data path override	216

Will Security be required to authorize Specific Users to control Retention and Backup Policies?

Storage policies can be used to distribute authority for data retention to different groups within your organization. Group level permissions can be assigned to each policy. This can be beneficial when different groups require different protection needs and due to business or government requirements authority must be granted to certain individuals within the organization.

Figure 7-8: *Defining separate storage policies and designating security to user groups responsible for defining policy settings.*

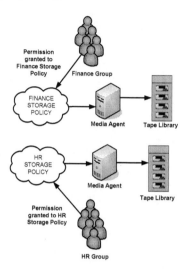

Determine Secondary Copy Configurations

Once the number of policies is determined you need to determine how many secondary copies will be required. Each storage policy will have a primary copy and any number of secondary copies depending on business needs. Each secondary copy can be uniquely configured to determine what data will be copied, how long it will be retained for, and what media it will be placed on.

Determine Number of Secondary Copies for each Policy

The number of secondary copies will be based on the locations of copies, retention of each copy, and what data (subclient association) will be placed on each copy. Secondary copies may be required for DR, data recovery, or archiving.

Disaster Recovery

DR copies may be required for on-site and off-site storage of data. It should also be considered that job placement on media may be critical to meeting RTO objectives. If four servers were backed up to the same tape to save media the servers can only be recovered one at a time. If the servers were placed on four separate tapes they could all be recovered at the same time by a four drive tape library. Although this would use more media, you could reduce the RTO for server recoveries. You can use multiple secondary copies and subclient associations to place specific jobs on media in proper sequence for recovery.

Data recovery

For data recovery needs, data may be required to be kept for extended periods of time. However, since data is mainly being kept on-site to meet these needs tape media can be left in the library and appended to until the tape is full. To maximize media usage, define subclients specifically for that data to avoid unneeded data from being kept longer then necessary. For data requiring different retention or media locations additional secondary copies will have to be created.

Data Archiving

Archiving of business data is usually required for business and government regulations. Time frequencies such as monthly, quarterly, or yearly are defined for archiving of data. This can be accomplished through the use of selective copies or extended retention rules. Create secondary copies based on archiving and retention needs. If data needs to be sent to different locations you will need secondary copies for each location. If different retention settings are required for archived data, additional secondary copies will need to be configured. Define subclients for data requiring archiving and use subclient associations to place data on correct media.

Figure 7-9: Secondary copies to provide disaster recovery, data recovery, and data archiving of logical business data

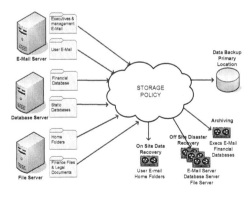

Determine Media Management Needs for Secondary Copies

When creating secondary copies one of the biggest advantages is the ability to consolidate backup data to media. This is done through the use of subclient associations and the combine-to-streams option. By defining data into logical subclients you can consolidate data onto media which will reduce the total space required for DR, data recovery, or data archiving needs.

Figure 7-10: Diagram illustrating four subclients associated to a secondary copy with combine to streams option set to 1.

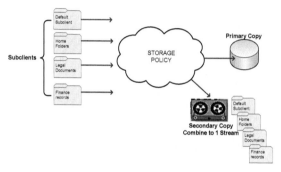

Figure 7-11: Diagram illustrating the use of subclient associations to consolidate data on media from different physical servers for media consolidation.

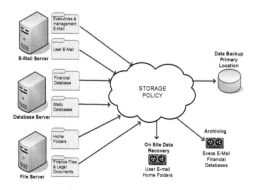

Determine Encryption Needs for Protected Data

Encryption can be used to secure sensitive data. This is especially critical when data is being stored off-site. CommVault offers in-line and off-line encryption options. In-line encryption can encrypt data on the client for secure transmission of data over the network or on the media agent for secure protection of data on storage. Off line encryption allows the flexibility to encrypt data after it has been backed up to primary media. The advantage of this is that backup time not be affected and data can be encrypted when auxiliary copies are performed to secondary media. The main advantage with CommVault encryption is that you can define data needing encryption into separate subclients. This limits the amount of data that needs to be encrypted and provides greater flexibility in managing encrypted data and its associated keys.

Figure 7-12: defining subclient for data requiring encryption and configuring off-line encryption to secondary copy.

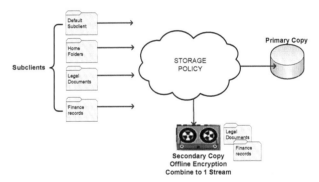

Policy Design Examples	Page
In-Line encryption for network and data security	194
Off-Line encryption for data security	196

Determine Settings for Storage Policies and Auxiliary Copies

The following section explains storage policy and auxiliary copy options. Refer to these tables when configuring storage policy settings. Each table contains the location of the setting in the interface, the option name, a description of the option and a reference to more information. For options described in this book, references to the correct pages are displayed. For options not covered in this book, refer to CommVault's online documentation for more details.

Storage Policy Settings

Tab	Option	Description	Reference
General	Device Streams	This is the number of streams used to write to the library. A general rule of thumb is to set this number to the number of drives (removable) or writers (magnetic) in the library.	Page: 38
	Incremental Storage Policy	This option allows you to link to another storage policy. Any incremental or differential backups will be written to the linked policy.	Page: 80
Copy Precedence	Copy Precedence	This determines the default copy which will be used first for browse and restore operations	See Online Documentation for more information
Security	Security	Determines which user groups have capabilities to manage the storage policy	See Online Documentation for more information on user and group security

Primary Copy Settings

Tab	Option	Description	Reference
Retention	Enable Data Aging	Deselecting this option will prevent data from aging and retain all data associated with this Storage Policy copy	See Online Documentation for more information
	Enable Managed Disk Space	Enabling managed disk will allow data to remain on magnetic media beyond the basic retention settings. Data will be pruned when the upper threshold setting is reached in the magnetic library configurations	Page: 77
	Spool Copy	For magnetic media this option will spool data to disk, copy to secondary media using auxiliary copy then delete data from the disk. Use this option when you have limited disk space but want to take advantage of fast disk write speeds.	Page: 79
	Basic Retention	Configure Cycles and Days settings for standard retention	Page: 55
	Data/Compliance Archiver Retention	Configure Days setting for Archive retention	See Online Documentation for more information
	Extended Retention	Extend basic retention for backup frequency of: all backups, weekly, monthly, quarterly, half year, and yearly backups. Up to three additional retention settings can be applied.	Page: 65
Data Path	Add	Allows you to add a new data path for the storage policy	Page: 21

	Delete	Allows you to remove a data path for the storage policy	Page: 21
	Set Default	Determines the default path data will use.	Page: 21
	Properties	Allows you to configure specific data path properties: Hardware compression, hardware encryption, chunk size, and block size	See Online Documentatior for more information
Data Path Configuration	Automatically Add New Data Path	This will automatically add new data paths when using a shared library	See Online Documentatior for more information
	Use Alternate Data Paths	Configure data path failover. Offline option is used if a library or Media Agent is unavailable. Resource busy can be used if all drives in a drive pool are being used.	Page: 21
	Round Robin Between Data Paths	This option will round robin data protection operations between multiple Media Agents. Note that this will not round robin individual streams for a job.	Page: 21
	Preferred Path	This is configured for LAN-Free data paths. Any jobs that do not have a LAN-Free path available will use the default path configured in the data paths tab.	Page: 21
Media	Enable Multiplexing	Determines the multiplexing factor. It is recommended to only set multiplexing when writing to removable media.	Page: 38 See Online Documentatior for calculation to determine ideal multiplex factor
Advanced	Data Verification	Data verification can be used to verify the integrity of chunks written to media.	See Online Documentatio for more information

Secondary Copy Settings

Tab	Option	Description	Reference
General	Primary Copy	This can be used to promote a secondary synchronous copy to a primary copy. When the synchronous copy is promoted the primary copy will be demoted to a secondary synchronous copy. All data associated with each copy will still be available for recovery	See Online Documentation for more information
	Combine to Streams	Determines the number of streams that will be used for the secondary copy. This will consolidate backup streams from all subclients associated with the copy and sequentially place the streams on backup media.	Page: 30
	Selective Copy	Designates this copy as a selective copy and enables the selective copy configuration tab	Page: 28
	Active	Designates the copy as active. If unselected data will not be copied. Any source data associated with the copy will ignore the associations and will prune when retention is exceeded.	See Online Documentation for more information
	Enable Inline Copy	This designates that a backup to the primary will also be written to secondary copies at the same time. Data from the client to the Media Agent can be written to multiple storage policy copies simultaneously.	Page: 44
	Defer Auxiliary Copy	This setting sets the number of days to wait before running the secondary copy. This setting should be used with caution as the wait interval will cause source data to remain on media the number of days the copy is being deferred regardless of the source data retention.	See Online Documentation for more information
	Calendar for Selective Copy	If custom calendars are defined this option will be available allowing you to select which calendar to use in regards to extended retention or selective copies. This is especially important when selecting time	Page: 84

frequency to create copies such as monthly, quarterly, or yearly.

	Default Destination	This is where the data path is defined: Library, Media Agent, Drive Pool, and scratch Pool. Once defined all options will be static except for the scratch pool which can be changed.	Page: 18
Retention	Enable Data Aging	Deselecting this option will prevent data aging from aging or pruning all data associated with the storage policy copy.	See Online Documentation for more information
	Basic Retention	Configure Cycles and Days settings for standard retention.	Page: 55
	Data/ Compliance Archiver Retention	Configure Days setting for Archive retention.	See Online Documentation for more information
	Extended Retention	This allows retention to be set as a Grandfather – Father – Son tape rotation. This option should only be set on secondary copies.	Page: 65
Copy Policy	Backup Selection	Determines the date that the secondary copy will begin generating copies. By default when a synchronous copy is configured it will attempt to make additional copies of all jobs that are currently retained. Setting backups on or after sets a start date which can avoid retroactive generations of previously run jobs. If using selective copy this option must be set to the specific date you want to start generating copies	See Online Documentation for more information
	Source Copy	Specifies the source location for the secondary copy. By default the primary location will be used as the source. A secondary synchronous copy can be selected to create other synchronous or selective copies. A selective copy can only be specified as a source for another selective copy.	See Online Documentation for more information
Data Path	Add	Allows you to add a new data path for the storage policy	Page: 21

	Delete	Allows you to remove a data path for the storage policy	Page: 21
	Set Default	Determines the default path data will use.	Page: 21
	Properties	Allows you to configure specific data path properties: Hardware compression, hardware encryption, chunk size, and block size	See Online Documentation for more information
Data Path Configuration	Use Alternate Data Paths	Configure data path failover. Offline option is used if a library or Media Agent is unavailable. Resource busy can be used if all drives in a drive pool are being used.	Page: 21
	Round Robin Between Data Paths	This option will load balance data protection jobs between multiple Media Agents. Note: This will not round robin individual streams within a job.	Page: 21
	Preferred Path	This is configured for LAN-Free data paths. Any jobs that do not have a LAN-Free path available will use the default path configured in the data paths tab.	Page: 21
Selective Copy	Automatically Select Full Backups at Frequency	Determines at what time interval full backups will be selected for copy. All fulls, weekly, monthly, quarterly, half year, and yearly fulls can be selected	Page: 28
	For each time period copy the:	Determines whether the first or last of time period will be selected. If selecting the last you can choose to select the most recent full that is scheduled or you can wait until the period is over before selecting a full. This can be useful when full backups must be performed when normal fulls are not scheduled such as the last business day of the quarter.	Page: 28
	Do not automatically select fulls	This allows the manual selection of fulls for the selective copy. You can use this with the select most recent full when auxiliary copy starts option in the general tab of the auxiliary copy settings	See the next section on auxiliary copy options

Associations		Allows you to select which subclients will be associated with the storage policy to copy to the secondary copy.	Page: 11, 29
Media	Mark media to be erased after recycling	Marks media to be erased after all data has aged from the media. This will only work if the Erase Spare Media option is enabled	See Online Documentation for more information
Advanced	Data Verification	Determines settings for data verification which is used to verify chunk integrity on the media	See Online Documentation for more information
	Data Encryption	Determines settings for data encryption. You can choose which algorithm and key length (where applicable) for the copy. You can also determine if you want to place the encryption keys on the media so data can be recovered using the Media Explorer tool	Page: 31 See Online Documentation for more information on Media Explorer

Auxiliary Copy Settings

Tab	Option	Description	Reference
Auxiliary Copy Options	All Copies / Select a Copy	Determines if all copies for the storage policy will be controlled by this auxiliary copy or just a specific copy	Page: 44
	Number of streams to copy in parallel	Determines how many devices (removable media drives) will be used when performing auxiliary copies. This option defaults to 1 so only 1 drive will be used. Once this number is set and the auxiliary copy options are closed it can not be changed.	Page: 45
	Start New Media	Forces a new tape to be loaded for the job. This can be used with mark media full to ensure certain jobs are isolated on media.	See Online Documentation for more information
	Mark Media Full	Once the job is complete the tape is marked full and no additional jobs will be copied to the media	See Online Documentation for more information

Job Initiation	Run Immediately	Job will be executed on demand.	See Online Documentation for more information
	Schedule	Job can be scheduled using the CommVault schedule.	See Online Documentation for more information
	Automatic Copy	Auxiliary copy will check at the set interval (default 30 minutes) to determine if additional data needs to be copied.	Page: 46
	Configure Alert	Allows you to set alert criteria specific to the auxiliary copy operation	See Online Documentation for more information

Advanced Auxiliary Copy Options

Vault Tracking	Export media after job finishes	Allows you to configure vault tracking options to export and track media automatically at the completion of the job	See Online Documentation for more information
Startup		Allows you to configure job priorities and job state that the job will run in	See Online Documentation for more information
Job retry		Allows you to configure the maximum running time and number of retry attempts for the auxiliary copy	See Online Documentation for more information

Storage Policy Design Flowcharts

The following section summarizes everything covered in this chapter into a series of flowcharts. Once you understand the concepts for storage policy design and implementation you can use these flowcharts as a quick reference point when designing your environment.

Summary of Design Steps

Determining Business Needs

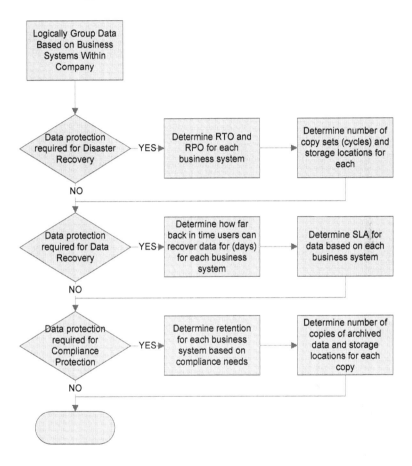

Storage Policy Design Based on Architecture

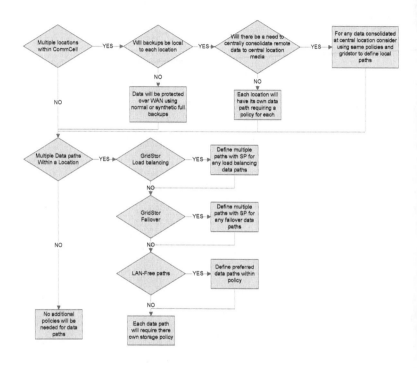

Design based on Primary Copy Location and Retention

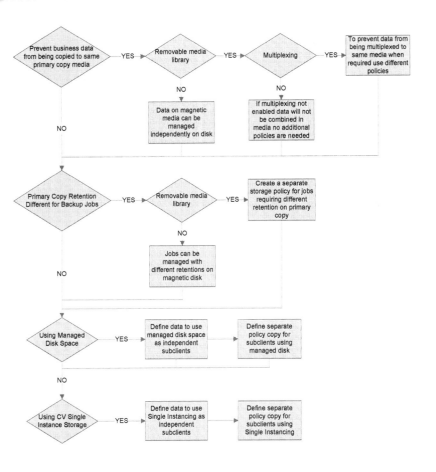

Policy Design Based on Security Needs

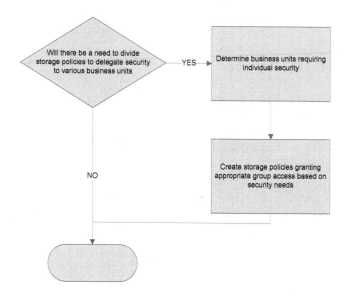

Number of Secondary Copies Required

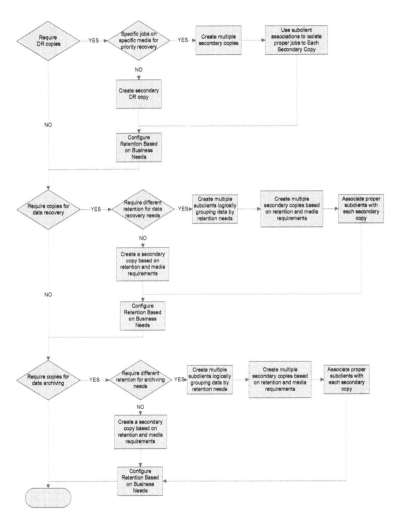

Media management Needs for Secondary Copies

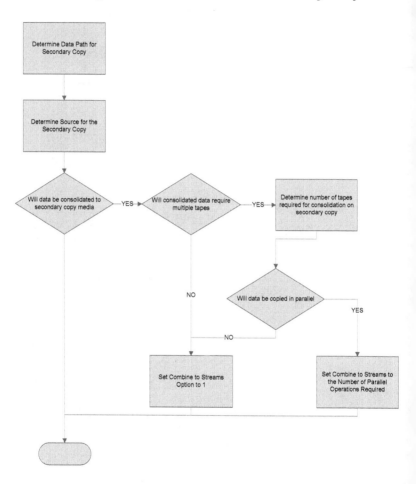

Encryption Requirements for Protected Data

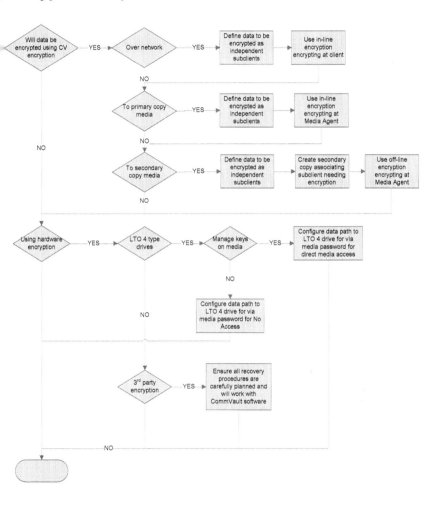

Determine Settings for Storage Policies and Auxiliary Copies

Determine Primary Copy Settings

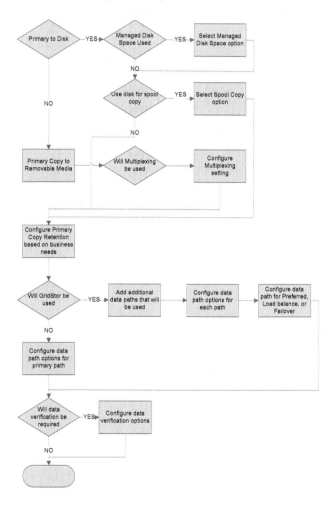

Determine Settings for Secondary Copy

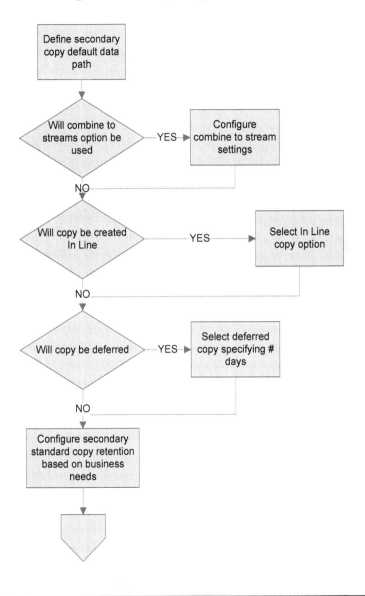

Determine Settings for Secondary Copy (continued)

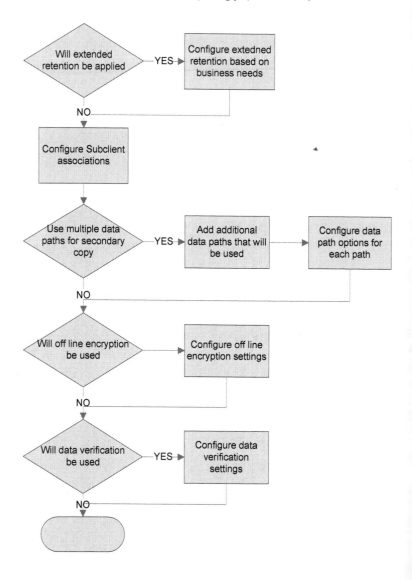

Determine Settings for Auxiliary Copies

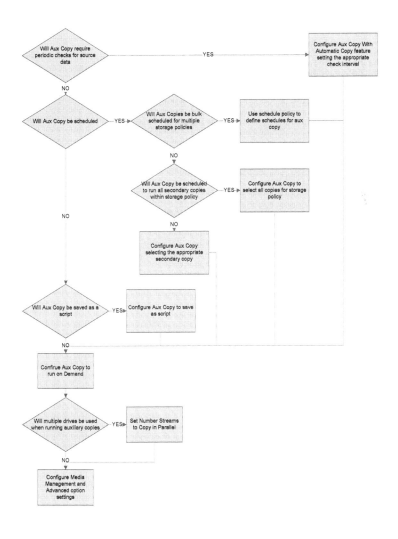

Part II CommVault® Solutions and Examples

Part II of this book is designed to provide real world solutions using CommVault® features. This section is NOT designed to be a step-by-step guide to creating storage policies and implementing CommVault Simpana® software features. Refer to CommVault documentation for step-by-step guides to learn more about configuring the CommVault environment.

Chapter 8- Storage Policy Case Study can be used as a starting point for designing CommVault solutions. It focuses on defining business goals, designing solutions to meet those goals, and implementing those solutions.

Chapters 9 -13 illustrate different examples of how CommVault features can be implemented to achieve a variety of business goals. Each chapter will contain a series of individual solutions that can be incorporated into any CommVault environment. Each example will contain two pages of information. The following summarizes the layout of the examples:

- A table detailing business needs, environment configuration, and solution will summarize the scenario.
- An implementation section will detail configurations within the CommVault environment.
- Screen captures from the CommCell® interface may also be inserted to illustrate methods for implementing the solution.
- A logical view will be diagramed representing the implementation from a CommVault perspective.
- A physical view will detail the environment layout
- The results section will highlight key points of the example and explain advantages and disadvantages of the solution.

Chapter 8

Storage Policy
Case Study

Chapter Summary
- Company overview
- Defining Business Goals
- Designing a solution
- Implementing solutions

The following chapter uses a fictitious company to illustrate the design and implementation of CommVault® software storage policy and retention strategies. The first part identifies business needs as defined by key decision makers within the company. The second part introduces technical aspects that will be incorporated into design strategies. The third part will focus on designing and implementing storage and retention policies. The last part will focus on implementation analysis. This section will also have page references to design examples from the last five chapters in the book which can be used as reference points to expand upon the basic case study design.

Company Overview

Widget Co. Incorporated manufactures and distributes electronic gadgets and wholesales them to other companies. Their main headquarters is in New Jersey and they have a west coast office located in California. They are a private company but intend on going public within the next two years.

Widget Co. has determined that a sound disaster recovery strategy must be implemented. Since they plan on becoming a public company they also want to start implementing data protection and archiving strategies to conform to Sarbanes-Oxley compliance standards.

A meeting of all key decision makers has been scheduled. It will include the CEO, CIO, and CFO as well as VP's and key managers. Technical managers, backup engineers, and key database administrators will also attend the meeting. Outside consultants and internal and external auditors will also be used to provide advice during the meeting.

Meeting Discussions

Key objectives are stated at the meetings to establish the following objectives:

- Sound Business Continuity strategy
- Disaster Recovery requirements
- Budgetary guidelines for implementing DR strategies
- Compliance issues and SOX requirements
- Time frames for implementing data protection strategies

All participants in the meeting advise on issues and state their concerns in their relative fields. Ideas from the meeting went in all different directions. To assist with notating key points of the meeting, keeping the meeting on track, and to allow for creative thinking with minimal boundaries; a mind map diagram was used to link key points.

Figure 8-1: *Mind map showing the thought flow of the meeting related to data protection and business continuity issues.*

Overall, several meeting were conducted providing excellent information that allowed for all parties involved to gain an understanding of company needs. Meeting results were noted and several charts were designed to better represent business needs. These charts will serve as the basis for all policy designs and implementations.

Business Meeting Results

The following section explains and details business needs in a series of charts. These charts are examples of methods that can be used to implement a data protection strategy.

Critical Business Systems

The meeting defined the following business systems as key components required for data protection. Each system is defined by its location and a description of the system. At this point only business systems are being considered. Technical aspects will be discussed later on.

Business System	Location	Description
Orders database	New Jersey & California	Two orders databases are maintained, one in NJ and the other in CA. Each one respectfully tracks orders for the East Coast and West Coast regions. The databases will interface with document repository for sales tracking.
Shipping Database	New Jersey	All shipping is coordinated through a central database managed in NJ. This database tracks inventory and shipping information which will be passed on from the orders database.
Administrative Databases	New Jersey	A series of administrative databases containing general information and HR data will be maintained in NJ.
Accounting Database	New Jersey	All accounting will be done in NJ. This is the central database for all financial information containing data for IRS and compliance.
Home Folders	New Jersey & California	User home folders will be local to each location.
Finance File Data	New Jersey	Along with the Accounting database will be a finance share containing spreadsheets and several small databases used by the finance departments.
Executives E-mail	New Jersey	Executives E-mail is maintained in a separate database on the mail server in NJ since they require different storage needs.
Managers E-mail	New Jersey	Manager E-mail is also maintained in a separate database on the mail server in NJ since they require different storage needs.

Users E-mail	New Jersey	All corporate users not in the Executives or managers groups will be maintained in several databases on the mail server in NJ
Sales Document Repository	New Jersey & California	The sales team enters sales information in forms linked in with document repositories in NJ and CA. These repositories are then linked to the orders DB.
Research & Development Document Repository	California	All company research is conducted in California and research data is maintained in a document repository containing research documents and research databases.

Protection Needs of Critical Systems

Data protection needs have been determined for disaster recovery, data recovery, and compliance. Being that the company plans on going public within the next few years it is critical that a sound data protection strategy be implemented. Because of this, management has allocated a higher budget to meet all protection and archiving needs. A data protection matrix table has been generated and approved by management as a starting point for developing data protection policies. The table is divided into disaster recovery, data recovery, and data archiving needs.

For Disaster Recovery, RTO and RPO (covered in Chapter 1) have been defined for critical business systems. The number of copy sets (cycles) to be kept on and off site have also been determined. A dedicated off-site disaster facility has been budgeted, and all DR media will be located at the facility.

Data recovery will not be needed for all business systems. User objects to recover are mainly for files, e-mail, and documents. Service Level Agreements, or time to recover, have been established for each business system. How far back in time users are able to request data recovery has also been determined which is illustrated in the chart as retention time.

It is agreed upon by management that the SLA recovery time can be altered if media capacity can not accommodate the quick recovery of all data. Every effort will be made to locate as much data on magnetic media as possible. This will simplify the recovery process for backup administrators and make for quicker recovery expectations of users.

For government compliance, and business and government requirements, it will be required that certain data be kept for long term archiving. For compliance data, the frequency interval that data will be protected for off-site archiving has been determined (noted in the off-site copies column). The length of time to retain the data has also been determined. Management has appropriated funds to store all archive media at a dedicated archiving facility. This is being done to comply with government regulations and ease the transition to becoming a publicly traded company.

Data Protection Matrix Table

Based on protection needs for DR, data recovery, and data archiving a matrix table has been constructed. The table focuses on each business system and the various data protection needs. This will serve as a transition point from business needs into technical needs. It will be the basis for storage policy design, retention strategies, and media capacity planning. The table will focus on the following needs:

Business Systems

Based on business meetings, critical systems are defined individually for protection requirements.

Disaster Recovery

For each business system an RPO and RTO have been designated. The number of copy sets or cycles to be maintained on-site and off-site has also been defined.

Data Recovery

The SLA for data to be recovered has been defined. This is the recommended time to recover user data when requested. The retention time has also been determined which is based on business decisions of how far back in time users can request the recovery of data.

Compliance

Archiving data for business and government regulations has been determined. For each business system the frequency in which data will be required to be archived and the length of time the data will be retained for have been defined.

Data Protection Matrix Table

Business System	Disaster Recovery			Data Recovery		Compliance	
	RTO	RPO	Copy Sets	SLA	Retention Time	Off-Site Copies	Retention Time
Orders database (NJ & CA)	4 hrs	1 hr	2 versions on 4 versions off	N/A	N/A	Quarterly	5 years
Shipping Database (NJ)	24 hrs	4 hrs	2 versions on 4 versions off	N/A	N/A	N/A	N/A
Administrative Databases (NJ)	48 hrs	24 hrs	2 versions on 2 versions off	N/A	N/A	Quarterly	5 years
Accounting Database (NJ)	48 hrs	4 hrs	2 versions on 4 versions off	N/A	N/A	Monthly Quarterly Yearly	1 year 5 years 10 Years
Home Folders (NJ & CA)	72 hrs	24 hrs	2 versions on 2 versions off	4 hrs	90 days	N/A	N/A
Finance File Data (NJ)	48 hrs	4 hrs	2 versions on 2 versions off	1 hr	6 months	Quarterly	5 years
Executives E-mail (NJ)	12 hrs	24 hrs	2 versions on 2 versions off	2 hrs	1 year	Quarterly	5 Years
Managers E-mail (NJ)	24 hrs	24 hrs	2 versions on 2 versions off	2 hrs	1 year	Quarterly	5 years
User E-mail (NJ)	48 hrs	24 hrs	2 versions on 2 versions off	N/A	N/A	N/A	N/A
Sales Document Repository (NJ & CA)	48 hrs	24 hrs	2 versions on 2 versions off	2 hrs	1 year	Quarterly	5 years
Research & Development Document Repository (CA)	48 hrs	4 hrs	2 versions on 2 versions off	4 hrs	90 days	N/A	N/A

Technical Aspects

Once business decisions are made, technical staff must work to implement strategies that adhere to company guidelines. This can often require reallocating resources or the purchasing of additional resources. Before storage engineers can determine if more resources are needed, an assessment of current resources and capacity will need to be performed. This will include current capacity to store data as well as projected growth of data over the next year. The following section explains the current architecture of the production and backup environments and how CommVault will be configured.

Environment Architecture

During the business meetings, focus was placed on business systems. The first step from a technical aspect is to associate the business systems with the servers and the applications they are running on. iDataAgents (iDA) will be installed on these systems to provide protection using application and file system API's.

From a technical aspect of data protection, focus must be placed on business systems and also be placed on core OS data as well. File System iDataAgents will be installed on all servers. This will allow for the protection of critical OS data and application program files. This data will be critical for disaster recovery purposes. The protection of this data will follow disaster recovery requirements based on the DR requirements for the servers the business systems are installed on as defined in the data protection matrix table.

Application agents will be placed on servers when required. This will allow for CommVault software to interact with the applications using their native API's. This will provide a great deal of flexibility in protecting data and simplify the backup process since it will not require application administrators to place applications in a state for CommVault software to protect the data. Any scripts or custom settings can be configured and applied in the data protection processes within the CommVault software.

The following chart illustrates how CommVault Simpana® software will interface with all servers and applications.

Location	Server	iDataAgent	Business System
New Jersey	Database Server	File System iDA	All OS and application program files
		Database iDA	Orders database
			Shipping Database
			Administrative Databases
			Accounting Database
			Home Folders
			Finance File Data
	Mail Server	File System iDA	All OS and application program files
		Mail iDA	Executives E-mail
			Managers E-mail
			Users E-mail
	Document Server	File System iDA	All OS and application program files
		Document iDA	Sales Document Repository
	File Server	File System iDA	OS and application data
			Home folders
			Financial file data
California	Database	File System iDA	All OS and application program files
		Database iDA	Orders database
	File Server	File System iDA	Home Folders
	Document Server	File System iDA	All OS and application program files
		Document iDA	Research & Development Document Repository

Physical Architecture

The company contains two locations: New Jersey and California. The two locations are connected by a high speed WAN connection.

New Jersey: Most servers and production data is located at the NJ office. A SAN has been installed to consolidate production data. The database server and the mail server are connected to the SAN and their production data is located on high performance redundant disks in the SAN. User home folders are maintained on the file server using Direct Attached Storage. The document server also uses direct attached storage for its document repository.

California: California has a Gigabit Ethernet production network with a file server and document server. All data storage is direct attached to the servers.

CommCell® Environment

There will be one CommCell® environment configured to manage both locations. The CommServe® server will be maintained at the NJ location. CommVault communication traffic will run over the WAN connection using the Robust Network Layer to ensure consistent communications and a minimal downtime in the event of network disruptions. All data will be protected locally to libraries in their respective locations.

New Jersey: Two dedicated Media Agents will be used to protect data being backed up over the production network. The mail and database server will have Media Agents locally installed to allow for LAN-Free backup data paths. All servers will have a file system iDataAgent and the appropriate application agents installed. A magnetic library and a tape library will be configured in the SAN to provide data protection for all NJ servers.

California: One Media Agent will be installed which will have a direct attached tape library. Each server will have a file system iDataAgent and the appropriate application agents installed.

Figure 8-2: *Diagram illustrating the Physical and CommVault architecture of Widget Co.*

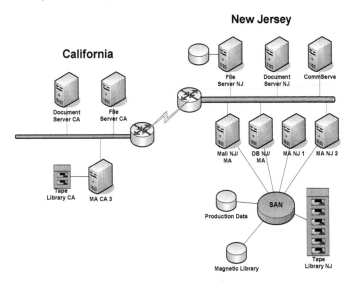

Data Size in Storage

Understanding capacity needs is critical to ensure proper data protection and to avoid running out of space. Careful consideration has been spent on analyzing the current environment and maintaining historical data to attempt to project the estimated size growth of data within the next year.

To better estimate and simplify media capacity planning, a chart has been generated showing each business system, the current estimated size, the estimated rate of growth and change, and the projected size of data within the next year. This chart will be used for media capacity planning and to determine if any additional storage capacity will be required.

Estimated Data Size Projected for 1 Year

Business System	Current Size	Rate of Growth	Rate of Change	Projected Size in 1 Year
Orders database	400 MB	25% Year	N/A	500 MB
Shipping Database	700 MB	30% Year	N/A	910 MB
Administrative Databases	60 GB	20% Year	N/A	72 GB
Accounting Database	100 GB	25% Year	N/A	125 GB
Home Folders (NJ)	750 GB	35% Year	4% Week	1020 GB
Home Folders (CA)	200 GB	35% Year	4% Week	270 GB
Finance File Data	150 GB	40% Year	3% Week	210 GB
Executives E-mail	100 GB	40% Year	N/A	140 GB
Managers E-mail	250 GB	40% Year	N/A	350 GB
Users E-mail	700 GB	35% Year	N/A	950 GB
Sales Document Repository (NJ)	75 GB	30% Year	25 % Week	98 GB
Sales Document Repository (CA)	30 GB	30% Year	10 % Week	40 GB
Research & Development Document Repository	300 GB	20% Year	25% Week	360 GB

Recovery Requests for User Data

Determining where data should be stored for data recovery will be based on the frequency of recovery requests. The following chart was generated from historical information for the past 2 years. It represents the percent of requests within 2 weeks, between 2 weeks to 1 month, and requests beyond 1 month. For database systems most data is requested almost immediately as the main purpose for protecting data is for data loss, corruption, or disaster reasons. User files, e-mail, and document recovery requests span well beyond 30 days. This is due to the flexible policies in place by the company. This is reflected in the data recovery retention times illustrated in the data protection matrix table.

User Recovery Requests of Historical Data

Business System	Recovery Requests Of historical Data in Days		
	< 14	14 - 30	30 +
Orders database	100%	N/A	N/A
Shipping Database	100%	N/A	N/A
Administrative Databases	90%	1%	9%
Accounting Database	90%	1%	9%
Home Folders	85%	10%	5%
Finance File Data	90%	8%	2%
Executives E-mail	1%	2%	97%
Managers E-mail	1%	2%	97%
Users E-mail	100%	N/A	N/A
Sales Document Repository	20 %	30 %	50%
Research & Development Document Repository	1%	6%	93%

Summary of Data Protection Needs

A chart has been generated based on the data protection matrix which specifies what media and how long data will be retained. This chart will be used to better estimate media capacity that will be required to meet business objectives by translating general retention requirements into CommVault retention settings based on cycles, days, and extended retention rules.

Due to the capacity of magnetic media at the NJ office all data will be backed up from the production environment to disk. To meet data recovery objectives a secondary copy to tape will be performed to keep data on-site for recovery. Off-site copies will also be made to tape for disaster recovery and data archiving.

Retention Settings Based on Data Protection Matrix table for on-site, off-site DR, and off-site archiving

Business System	Location	On-Site		Off-Site		Archive	
		Media	Retention	Media	Retention	Media	Retain
Orders Database	New Jersey	Daily Disk	(2,14)	Week Tape	(4,28)	Quarter Tape	(20,1825)
Orders Database	California	Daily Disk	(2,14)	Week Tape	(4,28)	Quarter Tape	(20,1825)
Shipping Database	New Jersey	Daily Disk	(2,14)	Week Tape	(4,28)	N/A	N/A
Administrative Databases	New Jersey	Daily Disk	(2,14)	Week Tape	(2,14)	Quarter Tape	(20,1825)
Accounting Database	New Jersey	Daily Disk	(2,14)	Week Tape	(4,28)	Month Tape	(12,365)
						Quarter	(20,1825)
						Year	(10,3650)
Home Folders	New Jersey	Daily Disk Tape	(2,14) (12,90)	Week Tape	(2,14)	N/A	N/A
Home Folders	California	Daily Tape Tape	(2,14) (12,90)	Week Tape	Week (2,14)	N/A	N/A
Finance File Data	New Jersey	Daily Disk Tape	(2,14) (24,180)	Week Tape	(2,14)	Quarter Tape	(20,1825)
Executives E-mail	New Jersey	Daily Disk Tape	(2,14) (52,365)	Week Tape	(2,14)	Quarter Tape	(20,1825)
Managers E-mail	New Jersey	Daily Disk Tape	(2,14) (52,365)	Week Tape	(2,14)	Quarter Tape	(20,1825)
Users E-mail	New Jersey	Daily Disk	(2,14)	Week Tape	(2,14)	N/A	N/A
Sales Document Repository	New Jersey	Daily Disk Tape	(2,14) (52,365)	Week Tape	(2,14)	Quarter Tape	(20,1825)
Sales Document Repository	California	Daily Tape Tape	(2,14) (52,365)	Week Tape	(2,14)	Quarter Tape	(20,1825)
Research and Development Document Repository	California	Daily Tape Tape	(2,14) (12,90)	Week Tape	(2,14)	N/A	N/A

Designing the Solution

To design a complete solution several storage policies will be needed to meet business goals. The policies will all have a standard naming convention starting with the location name, policy purpose, and other criteria specific to the policy. To simplify the protection and management of data, storage policies will be created specifically in line with business needs.

Data will be logically grouped in the production environment by defining business data as subclients. This will allow for the flexibility to manage protected data in the backup environment.

Defining Subclients

To meet business needs, subclients will be defined to protect data defined in the data protection matrix. This will allow for more flexible backup strategies and allow the logical grouping of data in the backup environment to consolidate business data, properly retain data, and locate data at the appropriate off-site locations. The following charts diagram the subclient configurations for the New Jersey and California locations.

The Default Subclient

A *Default Subclient* is automatically created for most iDataAgents when CommVault software is installed on a system. The Default Subclient has a unique feature as being a catch all for data the agent is responsible for protecting. The catch all will ensure that all data will be protected by the agent, even if more drives are added, paths are modified, or databases added. If the default subclient is modified or deleted the catch all feature will be disabled. The following charts will include the default subclient for all applications and file systems on each server.

New Jersey Servers, Applications, and Subclients

Server	Application iDataAgent	Subclient	Description	Approximate Size
File Server (NJ)	File System iDA	Default	OS, System State, and application data and catch all for additional data or drives added	20 GB
		Home	User data home folders	1020 GB
		Finance	Financial Spreadsheets and databases	210 GB
Database Server (NJ)	File System iDA	Default	OS, System State, and application data and catch all for additional data or drives added	20 GB
	Database iDA	Default	System databases and catch all for additional databases added	10 GB
		Orders		.5 GB
		Shipping		1 GB
		Admin		72 GB
		Accounting		125 GB
Mail Server (NJ)	File System iDA	Default	OS, System State, and application data and catch all for additional data or drives added	25 GB
	Mail iDA	Default	User e-mail and catch all for additional mail data	950 GB
		Execs	Upper management and executives	140 GB
		Managers	Middle management	350 GB
Document Server (NJ)	File System iDA	Default	OS, System State, and application data and catch all for additional data or drives added	25 GB
	Document iDA	Default	Catch all for any document repositories	50 GB
		Sales	Sales documents	75 GB

California Servers, Applications, and Subclients

Server	Application iDataAgent	Subclient	Description	Approximate Size
File Server (California)	File System iDA	Default	OS, System State, and application data and catch all for additional data or drives added	20 GB
		Home	User data home folders	
Document Server (California)	File System iDA	Default	OS, System State, and application data and catch all for additional data or drives added	25 GB
	Document iDA	Default	Catch all for any document repositories	
		Sales	Sales documents	

New Jersey Storage Policies

Several policies will be implemented to handle New Jersey backup data management. These policies will be implemented to take advantage of disk storage in an efficient manner to avoid large purchases to upgrade capacity. The policy design strategy will allow business goals for data protection to be achieved.

Since there is adequate magnetic disk capacity, all backups will be written to the disk library. Additional secondary copies will be created to meet disaster recovery, data recovery, and data archiving needs. Two policies will be used to protect data and maximize disk space.

NJ_DR_MAG policy will have a primary retention of (2,14). This policy will protect data mainly for DR and archiving purposes. Additional copies for off-site DR and archiving will be created to meet business retention needs.

NJ_DATA_MAG policy will have a retention of (2,14) and also have managed disk space enabled. This policy will protect data for DR, data recovery, and archiving. Since user data will be managed by this policy, the use of the managed disk space feature will increase the probability of recovering data from disk. Additional copies for on-site data recovery, off-site DR and archiving will be created to meet business retention needs.

NJ_DR_MAG Policy

Data will be logically divided into subclients on the four servers based on business requirements. This will allow for adequate protection needs based on the data protection matrix table. It will also allow for maximum media consolidation for on-site and off-site protection of data. Data directed to the NJ_DR_MAG policy is mainly for disaster recovery and archiving reasons. Data will be protected to magnetic media for primary backups then divided into secondary copies for disaster recovery and data archiving based on business needs.

Figure 8-3: *Diagram illustrating the four servers at the NJ location and subclient associations,*

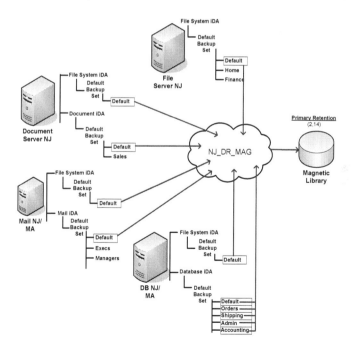

Secondary Copies for Disaster Recovery

To meet business requirements for disaster recovery, two secondary copies will
be created for off-site DR. Each one will associate subclients based on retention
requirements. These associations are based on the data protection matrix table.
Backup media will be located off-site at a dedicated DR facility. To meet
retention goals, two secondary copies will be required for DR:
Off_Site_DR_2_14 and Off_Site_DR_4_28.

Figure 8-4: Diagram illustrating secondary copies required for disaster recovery.

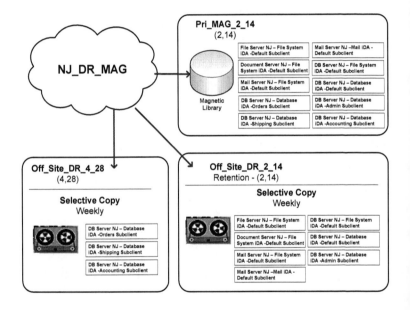

Secondary Copies for Archiving

Archiving data for compliance reasons will require two secondary copies. One copy will maintain data on a quarterly basis for five years. The other will maintain monthly data for one year with extended retention rules defined to keep quarterly backups for five years and yearly backups for ten years. Retention settings are based on the data protection matrix table. Data will be maintained at a dedicated archiving facility.

Figure 8-5: Diagram illustrating secondary copies required for data archiving.

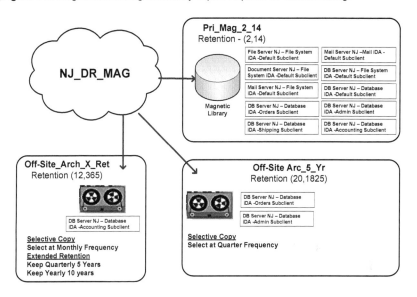

NJ_DATA_MAG Policy

The NJ_DATA_MAG policy will protect data for DR, data protection, and archiving. This policy will have managed disk space enabled. This will increase the potential of recovering data from disk for user data recovery. To maximize magnetic capacity two policies are being used so only data required for user data recovery will be set to use managed disk space. This does not guarantee the recovery of user data for the full time that historical data will be kept based on the data protection matrix table. As a result secondary copies will be created to maintain data on-site for recovery based on retention needs.

Figure 8-6: *Summary diagram of subclients associated with the NJ_DATA_MAG storage policy.*

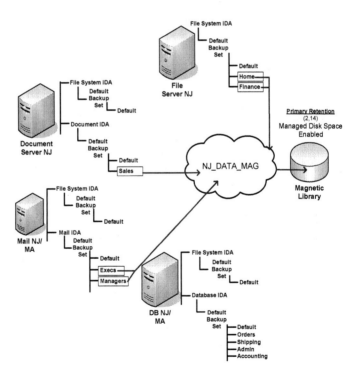

Secondary Copies for Disaster Recovery and Data Archiving

Two secondary copies will need to be created. The Off_Site_DR_2_14 will have all subclients associated with it for off-site disaster recovery. The copy will be a selective copy with a weekly frequency. The Off_Site_Arch_5_Yr secondary copy will be a selective copy with a quarterly frequency.

Figure 8-7: NJ_DATA_MAG storage policy with 2 secondary selective copies and associated subclients.

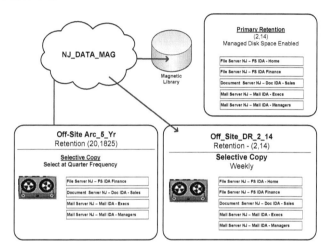

California Storage Policies

California will use one storage policy. All data will be backed up to the tape library as the primary location. Additional copies will be made for on-site data recovery, off-site disaster recovery, and off-site data archiving as needed.

The Off_Site_DR_2_14 secondary copy will have all CA subclients associated with it. It will be a selective copy with a weekly frequency. Two on-site secondary synchronous copies will be created. One will have 90 days retention and the other will have 365 days retention. An archive secondary selective copy will be created with a five year retention. This copy will be performed on a quarterly basis.

Figure 8-8: *Storage policy configuration with primary and secondary copies to meet California business system goals.*

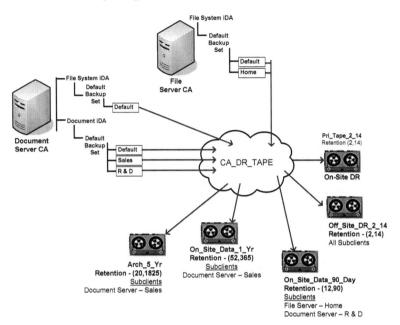

Media Capacity Planning

Business plans can only be carried out is there is adequate storage to retain data. Widget Co. currently has tape libraries in both locations and a magnetic library in the New Jersey location. Management has approved the purchasing of additional storage capacity if needed.

Current Libraries and Capacity

Location	Library	Capacity
New Jersey	Magnetic Library	15 TB
	Tape Library	LTO 3 6 Drives
		800 GB Each Drive
		50 slots
California	Tape Library	LTO 3 2 Drives
		800 GB Each Drive
		100 slots

Required Capacity for Magnetic Media (NJ)

Estimating the size of backup data to disk will be critical to ensure business requirements are met. Estimations of disk capacity have been created based on the estimated size of data per cycle multiplied by the number of cycles the data will be retained. The estimation in this case is based on 2 cycles.

Capacity for magnetic media in NJ

Business System	Estimated Size Each Cycle	Estimated Size in storage based on 2 cycle retention
Orders Database	500 MB	1 GB
Shipping Database	910 MB	2 GB
Administrative Databases	72 GB	150 GB
Accounting Database	125 GB	250 GB
Home Folders	1020 GB	2100 GB
Finance File Data	210 GB	450 GB
Executives E-mail	140 GB	300 GB
Managers E-mail	350 GB	700 GB
Users E-mail	950 GB	2000 GB
Sales Document Repository	75 GB	150 GB
Total size on magnetic media for 2 cycles		**Approximately 6 TB**

Required Capacity for Tape Media

To ensure adequate tape capacity, a table has been generated estimating the number of tapes that will be required to achieve business objectives. The table takes into consideration different storage policy copies since data can not be combined from one policy to another. The estimated number of tapes required to meet business goals assumes that once data on tape media has exceeded its retention, the media will be recycled back into the library and overwritten with new data.

Media Capacity Requirements for Tape Media

Storage Policy Copy	Size Per Cycle for all Subclients	Tapes Per Cycle 800 GB Capacity	Cycle Interval	Time Off Site / On Site (data recovery)	Estimated Tapes Required
NJ_DR_MAG					
Off_Site_DR_2_14	1140 GB	2	Week	2 weeks	8
Off_Site_DR_4_28	130 GB	1	Week	4 weeks	6
Arch_5_Years	75 GB	1	Quarter	5 years	22
Off-Site_Arch_X_Ret	125	1	Month	1 year	14
			Quarter	5 years	22
			Year	10 years	12
NJ_DATA_MAG					
Off_Site_DR_2_14	1800	3	Week	2 weeks	12
On_Site_90_Day	1020	2	Week	90 day on-site	26
On_Site_6_Mnth	210	1	Week	6 month on-site	8 *
On_Site_1_Yr	575	1	Week	A year on-site	40 *
CA_DR_TAPE					
Off_Site_DR_2_14	375	1	Week	2 weeks	4
On_Site_90_Day	40	1	Week	90 days on-site	2 *
On_Site_1_Year	30	1	Week	1 year on-site	2 *
Arch_5_Year	20	1	Quarter	5 years	22

* On-Site recovery media can be appended to until full. Number of tapes is estimate based on data size per cycle including incremental rate of change.

Configuring the Storage Policies

Once design strategies have been determined, storage policies can be defined. The following procedure outlines the steps to configuring storage policies and associating data with the policy

1. Define the storage policy
2. Define subclients
3. Associate subclients with appropriate policy
4. Configure secondary copies
5. Configure auxiliary copy operations using auxiliary copy or schedule policy to implement auxiliary copies

New Jersey Storage Policies

The following charts illustrate configuration settings for New Jersey storage policies, primary copy, and secondary copy configurations. Both policies will use 10 device streams writing to the magnetic library which has been configured for 10 writers.

NJ_DR_MAG (10 Device Streams)			
Subclients Defined to use Storage Policy	**Server**	**iDataAgent**	**Subclient**
	File Server NJ	File System iDA	Default
	Document Server NJ	File System iDA	Default
		Document iDA	Default
	Mail Server NJ	File System	Default
		Mail iDA	Default
	Database Server NJ	File System	Default
		Database iDA	Default
			Orders
			Shipping
			Admin
			Accounting
Pri_MAG_2_14	**Data Paths**	MA1_NJ → MAG_LIB (Default)	
		MA3_NJ → MAG_LIB	
		Mail_NJ → MAG_LIB	
		DB_NJ → MAG_LIB	
	Data Path Configuration	Round Robin between Data Paths	
	Retention	14 Days & 2 Cycles	

Off-Site_DR_2_14	Copy Type	Selective → Weekly		
	Data Path	MA1_NJ → Tape_Lib_NJ		
	Retention	14 Days & 2 Cycles		
	Combine to Streams	1		
	Subclient	**Server**	**iDataAgent**	**Subclient**
	Associations	**File Server NJ**	File System	Default
		Document Server NJ	File System	Default
		Mail Server NJ	File System	Default
			Mail	Default
		DB Server NJ	File System	Default
			Database	Default Admin

Off-Site_DR_4_28	Copy Type	Selective → Weekly		
	Data Path	MA1_NJ → Tape_Lib_NJ		
	Retention	28 Days & 4 Cycles		
	Combine to Streams	1		
	Subclient	**Server**	**iDataAgent**	**Subclient**
	Associations	**DB Server NJ**	Database	Orders Shipping Accounting

Off_Site_Arch_5_yr	Copy Type	Selective Quarterly Interval		
	Data Path	MA1_NJ → Tape_Lib_NJ		
	Retention	1825 Days & 20 Cycles		
	Combine to Streams	1		
	Subclient	**Server**	**iDataAgent**	**Subclient**
	Associations	**Database**	Database	Orders Admin

Off_Site_Arch_X	Copy Type	Selective Quarterly Monthly		
	Data Path	MA1_NJ → Tape_Lib_NJ		
	Retetnion	365 Days & 12 Cycles		
	Extended Retention	Keep Quarterly Backups for 5 Years		
		Keep Yearly Backups for 10 Years		
		Server	**iDataAgent**	**Subclient**
		Database	Database	Accountin;

NJ_DATA_MAG (10 Device Streams)

Subclients Defined to use Storage Policy	Server	iDataAgent	Subclient
	File Server NJ	File System iDA	Home
			Finance
	Document Server NJ	Document iDA	Sales
	Mail Server NJ	Mail iDA	Execs
			Managers

Primary Copy	Data Paths	MA1_NJ → MAG_LIB (Default)
		MA3_NJ → MAG_LIB
		Mail_NJ → MAG_LIB
		DB_NJ → MAG_LIB
	Data Path Configuration	Round Robin between Data Paths
	Retention	14 Days & 2 Cycles
		Managed Disk Space Enabled

Off-Site_DR_2_14	Copy Type	Selective → Weekly		
	Data Path	MA1_NJ → Tape_Lib_NJ		
	Retention	14 Days & 2 Cycles		
	Combine to Streams	1		
	Subclient Associations	Server	iDataAgent	Subclient
		File Server NJ	File System	Home
				Finance
		Document Server NJ	Document	Sales
		Mail Server NJ	Mail	Execs
				Managers

Off-Site_DR_4_28	Copy Type	Selective → Weekly		
	Data Path	MA1_NJ → Tape_Lib_NJ		
	Retention	28 Days & 4 Cycles		
	Combine to Streams	1		
	Subclient Associations	Server	iDataAgent	Subclient
		File Server	File System	Finance

On-Site_Data_90	Copy Type	Synchronous		
	Data Path	MA1_NJ → Tape_Lib_NJ		
	Retention	90 Days & 12 Cycles		
	Combine to Streams	1		
	Subclient Associations	Server	iDataAgent	Subclient
		File Server	File System	Home

On-Site_Data_6mnth	Copy Type	Synchronous		
	Data Path	MA1_NJ → Tape_Lib_NJ		
	Retention	90 Days & 12 Cycles		
	Combine to Streams	1		
	Subclient	**Server**	**iDataAgent**	**Subclient**
	Associations	**File Server**	File System	Finance

On-Site_Data_1yr	Copy Type	Synchronous		
	Data Path	MA1_NJ → Tape_Lib_NJ		
	Retention	365 Days & 52 Cycles		
	Combine to Streams	1		
	Subclient	**Server**	**iDataAgent**	**Subclient**
	Associations	**Mail Server**	Mail	Execs
				Managers

Off_Site_Arch_5_Yr	Copy Type	Selective		
		Frequency → Quarterly		
	Data Path	MA1_NJ → Tape_Lib_NJ		
	Retention	1825 Days & 20 Cycles		
	Combine to Streams	1		
	Subclient	**Server**	**iDataAgent**	**Subclient**
	Associations	**File Server**	File System	Finance
		Mail Server	Mail	Execs
				Managers

California Storage Policies

The following chart represents configuration settings for the California storage policy. It will be configured to use 4 device streams since there are 4 drives in the tape library.

CA_DR_TAPE (4 Device Streams)

All California subclient data will be associated with this storage policy

Primary Copy	Data Paths	MA3_CA → Tape_Lib_CA
	Retention	14 Days & 2 Cycles
	Multiplexing	Factor of 2

Off-Site_DR_2_14	Copy Type	Selective		
	Data Path	MA3_CA → Tape_Lib_CA		
	Retention	14 Days & 2 Cycles		
	Combine to Streams	1		
	Subclient	**Server**	**iDataAgent**	**Subclient**
	Associations	**File Server CA**	File System	Default
				Home
		Document	File System	Default
		Server CA	Document	Default
				Sales
				R & D

On-Site_Data_90	Copy Type	Synchronous		
	Data Path	MA3_CA → Tape_Lib_CA		
	Retention	90 Days & 12 Cycles		
	Combine to Streams	1		
	Subclient	**Server**	**iDataAgent**	**Subclient**
	Associations	**File Server**	File System	Home
				R & D

On-Site_Data_1yr	Copy Type	Synchronous		
	Data Path	MA3_CA → Tape_Lib_CA		
	Retention	365 Days & 52 Cycles		
	Combine to Streams	1		
	Subclient	**Server**	**iDataAgent**	**Subclient**
	Associations	**Document**	Document	Sales
		Server		

Off-Site_Arch_5yr	Copy Type	Selective → Quarterly		
	Data Path	MA3_CA → Tape_Lib_CA		
	Retention	1825 Days & 20 Cycles		
	Combine to Streams	1		
	Subclient	**Server**	**iDataAgent**	**Subclient**
	Associations	Document Server	Document	Sales
Off_Site_Arch_5_yr	Copy Type	Selective		
		Frequency → Quarterly		
	Data Path	MA3_CA → Tape_Lib_CA		
	Retention	1825 Days & 20 Cycles		
	Combine to Streams	1		
	Subclient Association	**Server**	**iDataAgent**	**Subclient**
		Document Server	Document	Sales

Configuring Auxiliary Copy Operations

Once the storage policies have been designed and configured, they must be
scheduled to run. This will be done through auxiliary copy operations. Auxiliary
copy operations can be set for a specific secondary copy, all secondary copies
within a storage policy, or for multiple storage policies using a schedule policy.
The following tables illustrate the auxiliary copy configurations that Widget Co.
will use to generate secondary copies.

NJ_Aux_Copy_wkly_Off			
Method for creating auxiliary copy	Schedule Policy		
Description	All auxiliary copies will be performed on Sundays and sent off-site on Monday morning. Since primary backup data is being protected to magnetic media, all drives in the tape library will be allocated to auxiliary copy operations.		
Settings	**Number of Streams to Copy in Parallel**	Allow maximum	
	Associated Policy Copies	Policy	Copy
		NJ_DR_MAG	Off_Site_DR_2_14
			Off_Site_DR_4_28
		NJ_Data_MAG	Off_Site_DR_2_14
			Off_Site_DR_4_28
	Job Initiation	Schedule	
	Schedule Settings	Day	Sunday
		Time	1:00 PM

NJ_Aux_Copy_Daily_On

Method for creating auxiliary copy	Schedule Policy
Description	Each night backups are performed using a standard weekly full and daily incremental schedule. During the day this auxiliary copy schedule will be used to update secondary copies to tape media for on-site data recovery
Settings	**Number of Streams to Copy in Parallel** — Allow maximum

Policy	Copy
NJ_DR_MAG	On_Site_Data_90
	On_Site_Data_6mnth
	On_Site_Data_1Yr

Job Initiation	Schedule
Schedule Settings	**Day** — Mon – Fri
	Time — 8:00 AM

NJ_Aux_Copy_Qrtr_Off

Method for creating auxiliary copy	Schedule Policy
Description	A schedule policy will be used to perform quarterly backups for off-site archiving. A schedule policy will be used here to simplify the scheduling process since each of the secondary copies are from different storage policies.
Settings	**Number of Streams to Copy in Parallel** — 1

Policy	Copy
NJ_DR_MAG	Off-Site_Arch_5_Yr
NJ_Data_Mag	Off-Site_Arch_5_Yr

Job Initiation	Schedule
Schedule Settings	**Frequency** — Monthly
	Last Sunday of Month
	Repeat Every 3 Months
	Time — 8:00 AM

NJ_Aux_Copy_Month_Off

Method for creating auxiliary copy	Auxiliary Copy Operation
Description	An auxiliary copy operation will be scheduled to run on the last Sunday of the month every month for monthly off-site archiving.
Settings	**Number of Streams to Copy in Parallel** — 1

Policy	Copy
NJ_DR_MAG	Off-Site_Arch_X_Ret

Job Initiation	Schedule
Schedule Settings	**Frequency** — Monthly
	Last Sunday of Month
	Time — 8:00 AM

CA_Aux_Copy_wkly_Off

Method for creating auxiliary copy	Auxiliary Copy Operation	
Description	All auxiliary copies will be performed on Sundays and sent off-site on Monday morning. Since primary backup data is being protected to magnetic media, all drives in the tape library will be allocated to auxiliary copy operations.	
Settings	Number of Streams to Copy in Parallel	2
	Associated Policy Copies	**Policy** **Copy**
		CA_DR_TAPE Off_Site_DR_2_14
	Job Initiation	Schedule
	Schedule Settings	Day Sunday
		Time 1:00 PM

CA_Aux_Copy_Daily_On

Method for creating auxiliary copy	Auxiliary Copy Operation	
Description	An auxiliary copy will be scheduled to run daily at 8:00 AM. This will be used to copy data to tape for on-site data recovery.	
Settings	Number of Streams to Copy in Parallel	2
	Associated Policy Copies	**Policy** **Copy**
		CA_DR_TAPE On_Site_Data_90
		On_Site_Data_1Yr
	Job Initiation	Schedule
	Schedule Settings	**Day** Mon – Fri
		Time 8:00 AM

CA_Aux_Copy_Qrtr_Off

Method for creating auxiliary copy	Auxiliary Copy Operation	
Description	An auxiliary copy operation will be scheduled to run every 3 months. This will be accomplished by setting the schedule to run on the last Sunday of the month and repeat every 3 months.	
Settings	Number of Streams to Copy in Parallel	1
	Associated Policy Copies	**Policy** **Copy**
		CA_DR_TAPE Arch_5_Yr
	Job Initiation	Schedule
	Schedule Settings	**Frequency** Monthly
		Last Sunday of Month
		Repeat Every 3 Months
		Time 8:00 AM

Solution Analysis

Implementing storage policies is only the first part to designing a complete
CommVault solution. Analysis must be conducted to determine the effectiveness
of the solution and where improvements can be made to better meet business
objectives while considering technical limitations.

The following chart breaks down and analyzes different aspects of Widget Co's
solutions. The chart contains analysis of each objective and a page reference to
other CommVault solutions which will be discussed in the following chapters
which can allow Widget Co. to better meet objectives.

Objective	Analysis	Advanced Solution
Backup Windows	It is difficult to determine during an initial implementation if backup windows will be met. For smaller backups and LAN-Free backups it may be possible that backup windows will be met. Widget CO. has determined that several critical backups are not meeting backup windows. They will use the following advanced CommVault solutions to better meet backup windows	Pages - 174 & 176
Recovery Time Objectives	Prioritized recovery of critical servers is a key aspect for Widget Co's data protection solution. Placing all OS data on the same media consolidates media usage but results in only 1 server being recovered at a time at a location. They will use the following advanced CommVault solutions to better meet backup windows	Page - 228 & 230
Recovery Point Objectives	Recovery Point Objective defines the maximum acceptable amount of data loss a company can have. RPO for most data for data loss will be 24 hours. Being that data is only being sent off-site once a week when secondary selective copies are created results in a 7 day RPO. In addition to that, several key databases have an RPO of 1 hour. This solution does not meet these needs. The following solutions can be implemented to meet RPO requirements.	Pages - 162 & 226
Media Management	Widget Co. is concerned by the time backups are taking at the California office. Duplicate backup data of the home folders, sales documents, and R & D documents are being kept on-site. Widget Co. is considering creating a separate storage policy for these subclients and setting the retention to 90 days.	Page - 166

Round Robin effecting Performance of Mail and DB servers	Round Robin load balancing can make backups more efficient by evenly distributing resources to backup jobs. For policy consolidation 4 data paths were defined in the NJ office for each storage policy. The problem with this is that occasionally backup data from the file server and document server are being load balanced through the mail or database servers. Widget Co. wants the advantage of consolidating storage policies and at the same time taking advantage of the round robin capability. The following solution using data path override can accomplish this goal.	Page - 216
Data Security	Data security will be a critical part of Widget Co's business objectives. Financial data and research and development data must be encrypted if being protected on removable media. For the NJ location data can be protected to disk without encryption then encrypted when being copied to tape using CommVault's off-line encryption solution	Page - 196
	For data being protected in California in-line encryption will be used since backups are going direct to tape.	Page - 194
Service Level Agreement	For data recovery needs, an SLA has been defined for different data. At the New Jersey location, storing data on magnetic media and using managed disk space improves the recovery time of user data. However at a certain point the data will not be available on disk and administrators will have to recover data from tape. One solution would be to use the disk to spool data during protection which will not be required for user data recovery. The data will then be auxiliary copied to tape and deleted. This will increase the available disk space for user data. The following solution implements CommVault's spool feature.	Page - 178
	Another solution that can be implemented is incremental storage policies. This can be used to direct full backups direct to tape and incremental backups to disk. This can also increase disk efficiency by not placing large full backups on disk but may slow down backup performance.	Page - 184
Ensuring Critical Backups are Successful	The R & D subclient has failed to backup several times due to library failures at the California office. Widget Co. wants to define a failover path for that data to backup over the WAN if no resources are available locally. This will require a separate storage policy to be defined and failover to be configured. The following CommVault solution explains how this can be accomplished.	Page - 214

WAN backups for data consolidation	Widget Co. is considering consolidating all backup data to the New Jersey location. They are considering performing WAN based backups taking advantage of CommVault's synthetic full feature. This will allow for better consolidation of backup data and consolidate media management requirements.	Pages - 202 & 206
Satellite offices	Widget Co. has plans in the next year to add several satellite offices. The offices will contain user data that must be protected but the WAN bandwidth will not be adequate to perform remote backups over the WAN. There will be no dedicated IT staff at these locations and a minimal investment in equipment will be made. Widget Co. wants to implement a solution to use USB drives which will be mailed to the main location on a weekly basis. The following CommVault solution will accomplish these goals.	Page - 204
Protection needs for archived data to match fiscal year	Widget CO's fiscal year begins on April 1st. Selection of backup operations to be archived off-site is using a standard January 1st fiscal calendar. The following solution will allow the company to define a custom calendar based on their fiscal year.	Page - 188
Auxiliary copy performance	Widget CO. has found that auxiliary copy performance is slow and underutilizing library resources. The following solutions can be implemented to increase the speed and resources used by auxiliary copy operations.	Pages - 190 & 192
CommServe protection	One aspect of data protection which has been overlooked (and is often over looked in real implementations) is the CommServe database backup. Every morning at 10:00, by default a backup of the CommServe SQL database is performed. This will be the essential component to recovering a CommCell environment. The following CommVault solutions can be used to securely protect the CommServe database.	Pages - 232, 234 & 236
Information Lifecycle Management	With growing sizes of e-mail and use data, Widget Co. is considering implementing a migration archive solution using CommVault software. They want to plan an ILM strategy for home folder data as well as develop an archiving solution for user e-mail to reduce production data storage requirements and reduce backup windows.	Page - 220
Security needs for data recovery	With the speed in witch Widget CO. is expanding and the increasing responsibilities for the IT staff, recoveries of user data will be delegated to a dedicated help desk group. To protect sensitive data, security must be set in place to limit what the help desk group can recover. Security needs to be set in place to allow the help desk group to only recover data from home folders. The following CommVault solutions will meet this goal	Page - 218

Case Study Summary

The case study was designed to provide basic guidelines and logic flow to design a storage policy solution. It serves as a simple example to show how Simpana software can be used to protect data for a variety of needs. This example is by no means the final configurations that will be performed for an environment. As shown in the solution analysis, aspects of performance, changing environments, new perceived risks, and long term goals will have to be considered to ensure a complete data protection strategy.

Though this case study can serve as guidelines for implementing a solution you should always check with professional services and other experts before implementing a complete CommVault solution.

Chapter 9

Basic Storage Policy Examples

Chapter Summary

- Single copy storage policy design
- Storage policy with weekly off-site copy
- Storage policy with daily off-site copy
- Multiple storage policies to divide business data
- Multiple storage policies to define different primary copy retention
- Multiple storage policies when using multiple Media Agents
- Grandfather, father, son tape rotation using extended retention

The following section provides scenarios for implementing basic storage policy configurations. It is intended to demonstrate designing real world data management solutions based on concepts discussed in section 1. This section is not a step-by-step guide to creating storage policies, as step guides are already available in CommVault's online documentation.

Single Copy Storage Policy Design

Business Needs	• Provide basic protection for 5 file servers. • Retain 2 cycles of data • Current cycle will be kept on site and previous cycle will be kept off-site
Infrastructure	• 5 physical serves running Windows 2003 Enterprise Server will be backed up to tape • Weekly fulls will start on Friday night • Incrementals will be run Monday through Thursday.
CommVault® environment	• A CommServe® / Media Agent server will be used with a 2 drive tape library direct SCSI attached • File system iDataAgents will be installed on each of the file servers
Solution	• One storage policy with a primary copy will be configured • The data path will point to the tape library • Retention will be set for 2 cycles and 14 days (2,14)

Implementation: A storage policy is created with a primary copy. Retention is configured for (2,14). Subclients for each server are associated wit the storage policy. Screenshot showing retention configurations in the storage policy copy.

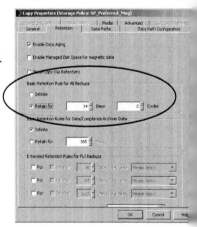

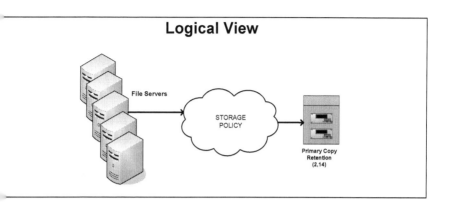

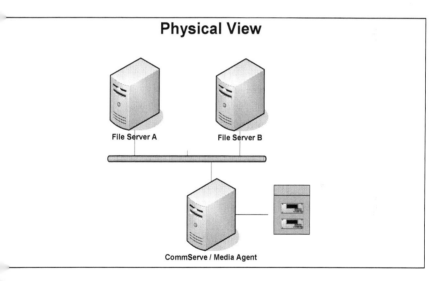

Results: This provides the very basic level of protection, keeping the current cycle on-site allows for recovery of data with an RPO of about 24 hours. In the case of a site disaster however the RPO can jump to 7+ days. CommVault recommends always having two copies of data, one on-site and one off-site.

Storage Policy Design for Weekly Off-Site

Business Needs	• Provide basic protection for 5 file servers. • Retain 2 cycles of data. • Weekly fulls and daily incrementals will be kept on-site. • A weekly copy will be sent off-site.
Infrastructure	• 5 physical serves running Windows 2003 Enterprise Server will be backed up to tape. • Weekly fulls will start on Friday night. • Incrementals will be run Monday through Thursday.
CommVault® environment	• A CommServe / Media Agent server will be used with a 2 drive tape library direct SCSI attached. • File system iDataAgents will be installed on each of the file servers.
Solution	• One storage policy with a primary copy and secondary selective copy will be configured. • The data path will point to the tape library. • Retention on both copies will be set for 2 cycles and 14 days (2,14)

Implementation: A storage policy is created with a primary and a secondary selective copy. Retention is configured for each copy for (2,14). Subclients for all servers are associated with the selective copy allowing for data consolidation. Combine to streams option is set to 1. Screenshot showing selective full options.

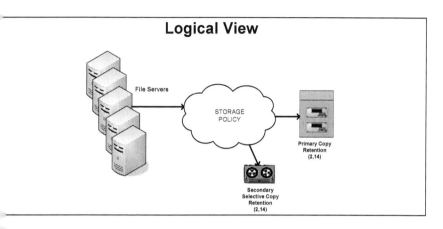

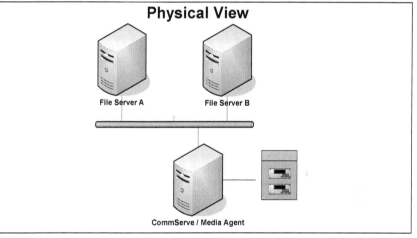

Results: This provides the on-site and off-site protection of data. Depending on how often you send tapes off-site will determine your Recovery Point Objective (RPO)

Storage Policies with Daily Off-Site Copy

Business Needs	• Provide data protection for 2 file servers • Provide daily off-site protection for all data
Infrastructure	• 2 file servers
CommVault® environment	• CommServe/Media Agent with direct attached tape library
Solution	• Create a storage policy with a primary and secondary synchronous copy • Schedule auxiliary copy operations to run daily

Implementation: A storage policy is configured with a primary and secondary synchronous copy. All subclients are associated with the storage policy. Secondary synchronous copy is configured selecting all subclients in the associations tab. Auxiliary copy is then scheduled selecting the secondary copy to run daily.

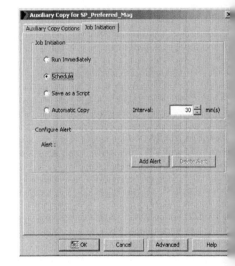

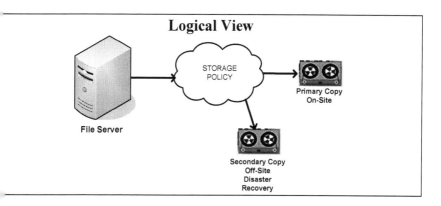

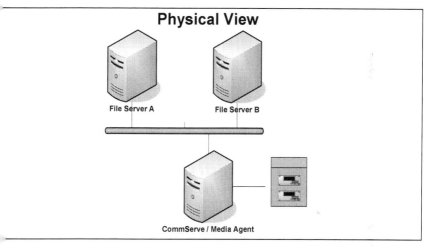

Results: This method of protection provides daily off-site protection of data providing a 24 hour RPO. This solution provides strong basic protection and accomplishes the goal of always having on-site and off-site protection.

Multiple Storage Policies to Separate Business Data in the Primary Location

Business Needs	• Protect file system data to be kept on-site and off-site for disaster recovery • Protect database data for on-site and off-site DR and off-site archiving • Avoid multiplexing data to the same media
Infrastructure	• File server and database server
CommVault® environment	• CommServe server, Media Agent and a tape library
Solution	• Create two storage policies. • File server subclients point to one policy and database server points to the other

Implementation: Two storage policies are created. The first one is dedicated to the file server and the second to the database server. Multiplexing factor is set to 3. Additional secondary copies are created for each storage policy for off-site data storage. You can use the *Associated Subclients* tab to view which subclients are associated with a storage policy.

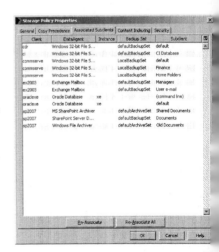

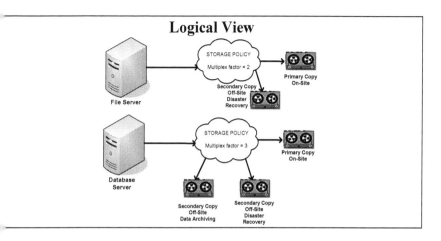

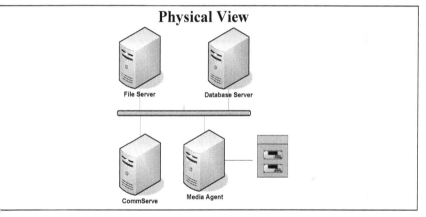

Results: This solution is effective at dividing logical business data. In this case two storage policies are created so specific business data will be written to the appropriate media. This is more important when multiplexing to tape since data from different servers are prevented from being mixed to media. Since storage policy copies own associated media, the database and file system data will never be combined to the same media.

Multiple Storage to define different primary retention settings

Business Needs	• Provide on-site and off-site disaster recovery for a file server for a standard retention of (2,14) • Provide on-site disaster recovery and mail recovery for a mail server for retention of (4,28) • Provide off-site disaster recovery for all data for 4 cycles and 28 days
Infrastructure	• File server and Mail server
CommVault® environment	• CommServe server, Media Agent and a disk library
Solution	• Create two storage policies. • Create a file server storage policy and set primary copies retention to (2,14) • Create a Mail server storage policy and set primary copies retention to (4,28)

Implementation: Two storage policies have been created. The File Server policy has a primary copy with a (2,14) retention and an secondary copy with a (4,28) retention. The second copy has a primary copy and a secondary copy with a (4,28) retention. The Storage Device tab in the subclient properties is used to associate the subclient with a storage policy.

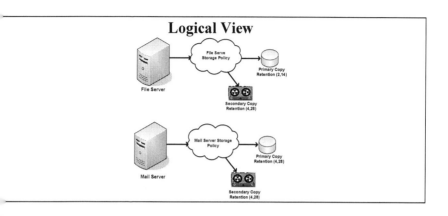

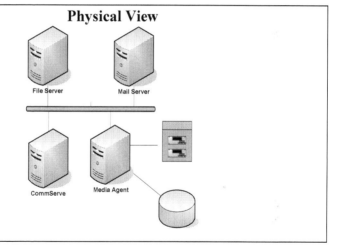

Results: This is an illustration of creating multiple storage policies when the primary copy location needs to have different retention settings. The data is physically being stored on the same magnetic library but logically it is being managed through different storage policies.

Multiple Storage Policies Using Multiple Media Agents

Business Needs	• Provide backups for several file and mail servers • Balance backups by directing file servers to one Media Agent and mail servers to the other
Infrastructure	• Several file and mail servers with direct attached storage
CommVault® environment	• CommServe server • 2 Media Agents with direct attached tape libraries
Solution	• Define 2 storage policies each defining a data path to the appropriate Media Agent and library

Implementation: For this example 2 storage policies will be needed to define 2 data paths. Each Media Agent will have its own library and require its own data path. Note that this example illustrates the use of two storage policies to define 2 paths, but this can also be accomplished using GridStor™ Technology which will be discussed in the Enterprise Design Examples chapter.

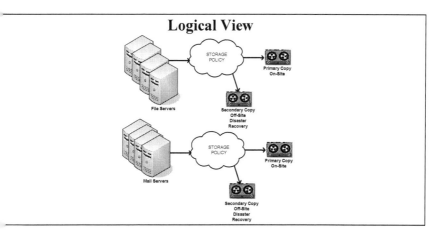

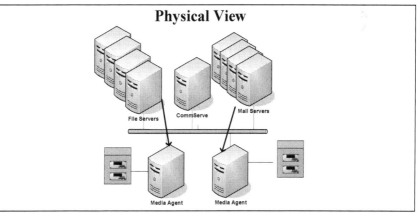

Results: Directing jobs to the appropriate Media Agent and library allows you to take advantage of balancing data protection operations. This can also be accomplished by using GridStor technology with its Round-Robin load balancing feature.

Setting a Grandfather-Father-Son Tape Rotation Using Extended Retention

Business Needs	<ul><li>Provide on-site data protection for 2 cycles and 14 days</li><li>Keep monthly fulls off-site for a year</li><li>Keep quarterly fulls off-site for 5 years</li><li>Keep yearly fulls off-site infinitely</li></ul>
Infrastructure	• Small office with several file servers
CommVault® environment	<ul><li>CommServe server, Media Agent, and a tape library</li><li>File servers have file system iDataAgent</li></ul>
Solution	<ul><li>Configure standard retention for (2,14)</li><li>Configure extended retention to keep:<ul><li>Monthly fulls for 1 year</li><li>Quarterly fulls for 1825</li><li>Yearly fulls for Infinite</li></ul></li></ul>

Implementation: Configure the Extended retention as shown in the following screen shot. The result will extend the retention of the appropriate monthly, quarterly and yearly full backups.

Physical chart showing tape rotation scheme using extended retention rules.

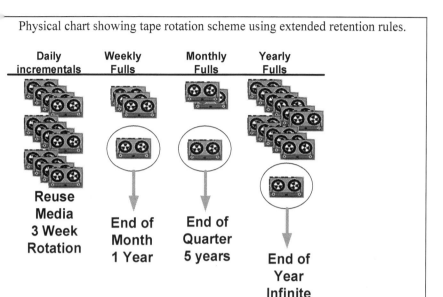

Results: Extended retention rules extend the retention of full backups meeting certain criteria. This can be an effective method of managing more complex tape rotation schemes. It is strongly recommended that you do not set extended retention rules to the primary copy. Instead create a secondary copy and apply the extended retention rules to that copy.

Chapter 10

Advanced Storage Policy Examples

Chapter Summary
- Creating and managing multiple subclients
- Multi-streaming subclient backups
- Spooling to magnetic media
- Specifying source for Auxiliary Copy
- Logically managing data through subclient associations
- Incremental storage policies
- Managed disk space
- Custom business calendars
- Using drive pools
- Designating Number of drives using auxiliary copy
- In-line and off-line encryption

The following section provides advanced CommVault® software design strategies. These strategies improve upon the examples discussed in the basic examples chapter and the case study chapter. Strategies to improve backup performance, manage media more efficiently, and allocate backup resources will be discussed.

Creating Multiple Subclients to divide home folders

Business Needs	• Provide faster backups for home folders
Infrastructure	• File server with home folder data on a large disk array
CommVault® environment	• CommServe® server, Media Agent and appropriate iDataAgent installed on each server
Solution	• Create two subclients dividing home folder data based on first letter of users folder name

Implementation: Subclient content can be defined using regular expressions (wildcards) allowing you to dynamically map a large number of folders to different subclients. In this example the home folders are divided into two subclients \home folders\[A-M]* and \home folders\[N-Z]*. The bracketed letter range identifies folders beginning with that letter while the asterisk identifies any number of characters in the folder name. Use of wildcards when defining subclient content allows automatic assignment of new folders to the appropriate subclient. The alternative is to define content at a common parent level which gives you no division of content or to statically enter each folder name and manually maintain the content.

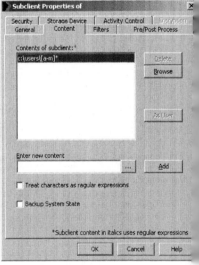

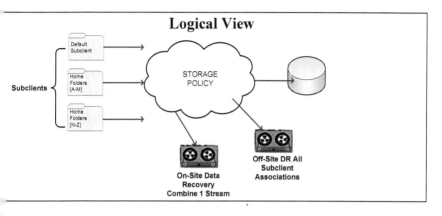

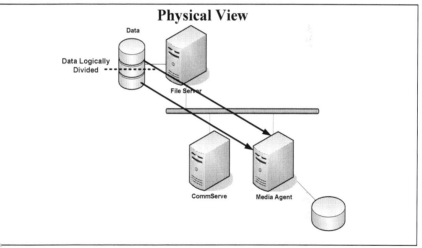

Results: The ability to logically divide folders through the use of wildcards adds a great deal of flexibility. In this case dividing the home folders location into two separate subclients allows you to multistream backup data and stagger schedule the backup jobs. The next example will improve on this idea by multistreaming each subclient when backing up.

Multi-Streaming Subclient Backup Data

Business Needs	• Provide faster backups of home folder data by dividing home folders into two subclients • Maximize backup performance by multistreaming home folder backups of high speed RAID array
Infrastructure	• File server with home folder data on a large disk array
CommVault® environment	• CommServe server, Media Agent and appropriate iDataAgent installed on each server
Solution	• Create two subclients dividing home folder data based on first letter of users folder name • Set each subclient to backup using 3 streams to take advantage of fast RAID read access

Implementation: Like the previous example the home folders are divided into two subclients. Since the home folder data resides on fast read access disks increasing the data readers to 3 for each subclient can improve performance even more. The option to allow multiple readers within a drive or mount point must also be enabled since multiple physical disks are logically being addressed by a single drive letter. Stagger scheduling the subclients to backup will result in two separate three stream backup of home folder data. Defining a secondary copy with a combine to 1 stream option will then take the 6 streams from the 2 subclient backups and consolidate the data to a single tape.

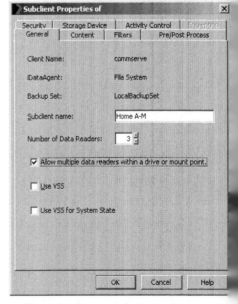

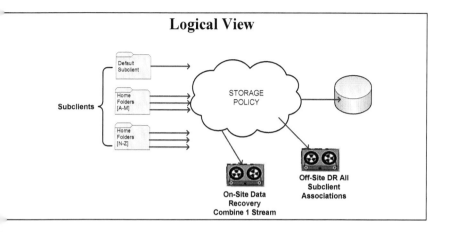

Logical View

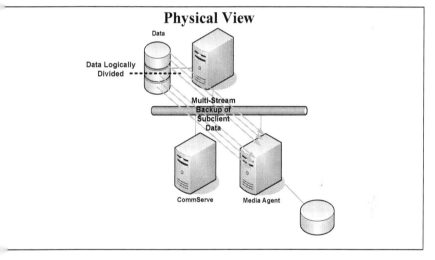

Physical View

Results: This solution builds on the previous example of dividing subclient using wildcards. In this example multistreaming each subclient and stagger scheduling the backup operations can improve backup performance as well as read performance from the source disks.

Spooling to Magnetic Media

Business Needs	• Meet backup windows by backing up to disk • Use the magnetic library for backups although it has limited capacity • Isolate backup data for each server onto its own media
Infrastructure	• File, database, and mail server • Magnetic disk library with limited capacity • Tape library
CommVault® environment	• CommServe server, Media Agent and appropriate iDataAgent installed on each server
Solution	• Configure a storage policy with a primary copy to the magnetic library. Set the retention for *Spool Copy*. • Create three secondary copies associating the correct subclient data from each server to the appropriate secondary copy

Implementation: One storage policy is used to backup all servers. The retention is configured to Spool Copy (No Retention). Secondary copies are created to isolate each server on different media. Screenshot showing the *Spool Copy* option.

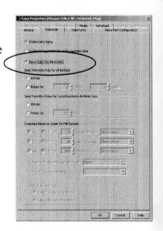

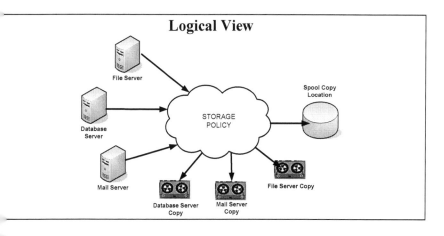

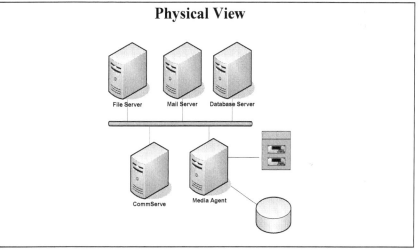

Results: By spooling to a Magnetic Library you can take advantage of fast disk storage and increased streams written to media. When there is limited disk capacity using the spool copy option basically sets a (0,0) retention. The data will remain on the disk until the secondary copy is successfully finished. The data in the primary location will then be deleted making space for new backup jobs.

Specifying Source of Secondary Copy

Business Needs	• Perform full backups on Friday and incrementals all other days
	• Spool all copies to disk for faster backups
	• Create an auxiliary copy of the Friday full on Sunday to send off-site
Infrastructure	• Several file servers
	• Magnetic library and tape library
CommVault® environment	• CommServe server, Media Agent and appropriate iDataAgent installed on each server
Solution	• Design a storage policy with a primary and two secondary copies
	• Configure a secondary synchronous copy to Aux copy data every day
	• Configure a selective copy specifying the secondary synchronous as the source copy

Implementation: Spooling to disk can improve performance of backup operations. In this example a full is being performed to a spooled disk on Friday. The Auxiliary Copy is being performed on Sunday. This means that regardless of the retention settings, the data on the disk will remain there until the auxiliary copy is run.

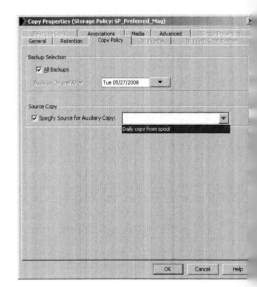

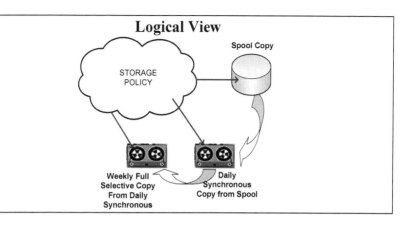

Logical View

STORAGE POLICY

Spool Copy

Weekly Full
Selective Copy
From Daily
Synchronous

Daily
Synchronous
Copy from Spool

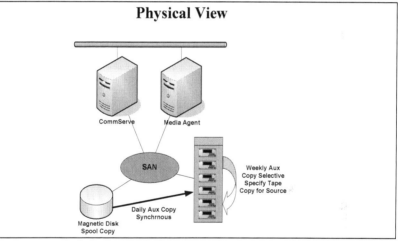

Physical View

CommServe

Media Agent

SAN

Weekly Aux
Copy Selective
Specify Tape
Copy for Source

Magnetic Disk
Spool Copy

Daily Aux Copy
Synchrnous

Results: Retention variants can affect the aging of data. In this case spooling to isk sets a (0,0) retention. However if a secondary copy relies on the spool as ne source, regardless of the retention the data will not be pruned from the disk ntil the secondary copy is copied. Since the weekly synchronous copy runs on unday, but the full backup runs to disk on Friday you should not use the spool)cation as the source. Specifying the synchronous copy as the source will allow ne data to properly age and be pruned from the spool copy on disk.

Logically Managing data Through Subclient associations

Business Needs	• More efficiently manage media by logically grouping data to media based on its storage needs:
	   o On-site recovery of E-mail and home folders for 90 days
	   o Off-site disaster recovery of all servers for 4 cycles and 28 days
	   o Off-site archiving of executives mail, financial databases, and financial and legal files for infinite retention

Infrastructure	• Mail, Database, and File Server
CommVault® environment	• CommServe server, Media Agent • Appropriate iDataAgent installed on each server
Solution	• Define subclient data in the production environment based on logical business needs • Create a storage policy with a primary copy writing to a magnetic library • Create additional copies and associate the proper subclient data within each copy

Implementation: By logically dividing data on production servers into different subclients, the data can be managed independently in the backup environment. Use the Associations tab in the storage policy copy to determine which data will be sent to each secondary copy.

---

http://www.commvault.com/training

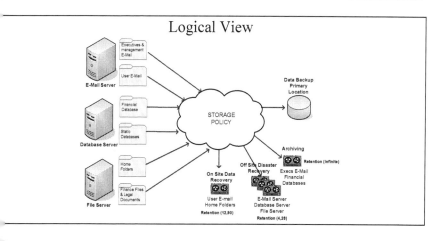

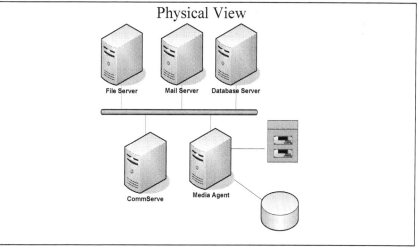

Results: Logically managing data by grouping like-data on a server into subclients results in independent management of that data in the backup environment. In this case media usage is greatly reduced by only placing needed data on specific media to meet business goals. This is what is called a Three Dimensional storage policy.

Incremental Storage Policies to Improve Backup Times and Disk Usage

Business Needs	• Decrease recovery times for user data by storing data on disk when possible • Recovery of home folder data is defined for 90 days
Infrastructure	• File server with home folders • Magnetic disk and tape library
CommVault® environment	• CommServe server, Media Agent, and a magnetic library • File server with File System iDataAgent

Solution	• Configure two subclients on the file server
	    ○ Default subclient for all OS, application, and system state data
	    ○ Home subclient mapped to all user data
	• Configure 2 storage policies
	    ○ SP_1 standard retention default subclient associated
	    ○ SP_2 standard retention with managed disk space enabled Home Subclient associated

Implementation: Two storage policies are created and linked together using the Incremental Storage Policy link (shown in screenshot) in the properties of the storage policy. Full backups will be performed to tape and incrementals to disk

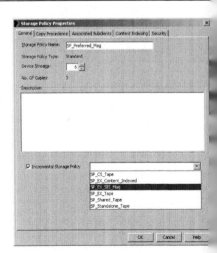

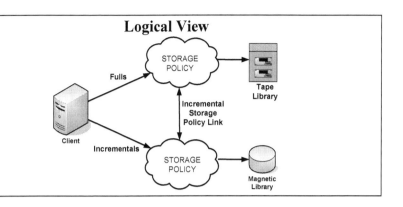

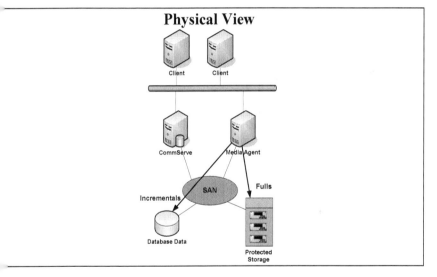

Results: Though incremental storage policies add a level of complexity to the backup environment they can also add great flexibility to managing data and media. Running incrementals to disk allows for faster backups and quicker recoveries of data. Backing up fulls to tape during the weekend allows better media management since the large full backups do not need to be managed by the disk storage.

Using Managed Disk Space to Improve Disk Storage Capacity

Business Needs	• Decrease recovery times for user data by storing data on disk when possible • Recovery of home folder data is defined for 90 days
Infrastructure	• File server with home folders
CommVault® environment	• CommServe server, Media Agent, and a magnetic library • File server with File System iDataAgent

Solution	• Configure two subclients on the file server
	   o Default subclient for all OS, application, and system state data
	   o Home subclient mapped to all user data
	• Configure 2 storage policies
	   o SP_1 standard retention default subclient associated
	   o SP_2 standard retention with managed disk space enabled Home Subclient associated

Implementation: Two storage policies are created. The first one provides basic protection for OS, application, and system data. This data is protected for disaster recovery and only needs to be retained for the minimum 2 cycles and 14 days. The second policy will protect user data. Managed disk space is enabled for this copy increasing the chances of data recovery from disk. However this does not guarantee recovery from disk and a secondary copy is created using (12,90) retention.

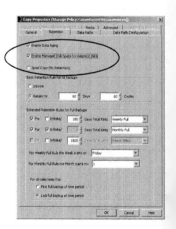

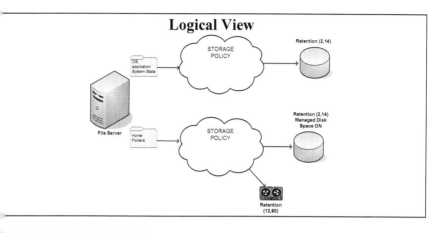

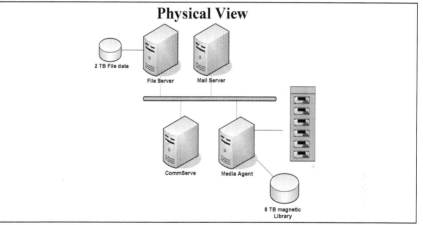

Results: The Home folders subclient is being directed to a different storage policy then the Default subclient. Though both subclients are physically stored on the same disk they are logically managed through different storage policies. This allows different retention to be configured and in this case managed disk space enabled on one of the copies. It is important to note that managed disk space increased the potential to recover data from disk but the secondary copy retained for 90 days must be configured to guarantee recovery of data to meet the business needs established.

Custom Business Calendars to Define Fiscal Year

Business Needs	• Define custom business calendar based on a fiscal year beginning March 1st • Send quarterly backups off-site for 5 years • Send yearly backups off-site infinitely
Infrastructure	• Several database servers requiring protection for disaster recovery an compliance
CommVault® environment	• CommServe server, Media Agent • Appropriate agents installed on servers
Solution	• Define a custom business calendar starting on March 1st • Assign the custom calendar to secondary storage policy copies

Implementation: A storage policy is created with a primary and secondary synchronous copy. A custom fiscal calendar is defined in Control Panel to match the corporate fiscal calendar. Option to make the calendar the default is selected.

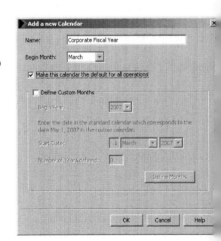

Results: Custom business calendars can be used to meet archiving goals by custom defining fiscal years. Custom calendars are defined in the control panel. You can then select which custom calendar to use within the storage policy copy. This adds great flexibility and you can also define different calendars for different needs. If you want to use one custom calendar for your entire CommCell architecture you can select the option *Make this calendar the default for all* operations.

Using Drive Pools to Allocate Library Resources

Business Needs	• Ensure that primary backup jobs have enough drives available for backups • Ensure that auxiliary copy jobs always have drives available even if primary backups are running
Infrastructure	• Several production servers backing up to a tape library
CommVault® environment	• CommServe server & Media Agent with a 6 drive library
Solution	• Define 2 drive pools for the library • 4 drive pool will be used for primary backups • 2 drive pool will be used for auxiliary copies

Implementation: 2 drive pools are configured for the tape library. A storage policy is created with a primary and secondary copy. In the data path of the primary copy the 4 drive pool is selected. For the data path of the secondary copy the 2 drive pool is selected.

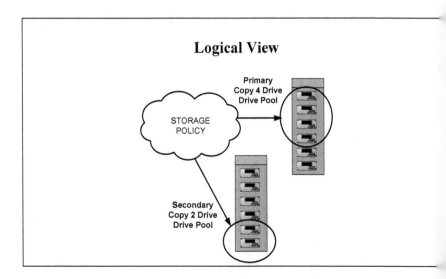

Logical View

STORAGE POLICY

Primary Copy 4 Drive Drive Pool

Secondary Copy 2 Drive Drive Pool

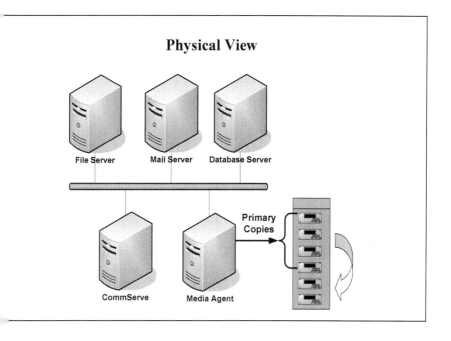

Physical View

Results: By logically dividing a tape library into drive pools you designate in the storage policy copy data path which pool you want to use. The advantage of this is that you can determine which resources will be used for certain jobs. In this case by creating a 2 drive pool for auxiliary copies you will ensure that auxiliary copies will always run and not be preempted by primary backup jobs.

Designating the Number of Drives for Auxiliary Copy Operations

Business Needs	• Ensure that primary backups have enough drives to run backups
	• Dedicate 2 drives in the library to auxiliary copies and ensure that primary backups will not interrupt auxiliary copies when running
Infrastructure	• Several production servers backing up to a tape library
CommVault® environment	• CommServe server & Media Agent with a 6 drive library
Solution	• Ensure that backups Preempt Auxiliary Copies option is deselected
	• Set Number of streams to copy in parallel is set to 2

Implementation: Job Preemption control in Job Management can be used as a master on off switch for job preemption. Backup jobs have a higher priority than an auxiliary copy job and, depending on CommVault® software configurations, can interrupt auxiliary copies while running. The option is deselected (by default) to ensure auxiliary copies will not be interrupted. Setting the number of streams to copy in parallel to 2 will result in 2 drives being dedicated to the auxiliary copy operation.

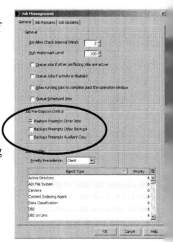

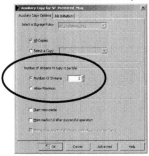

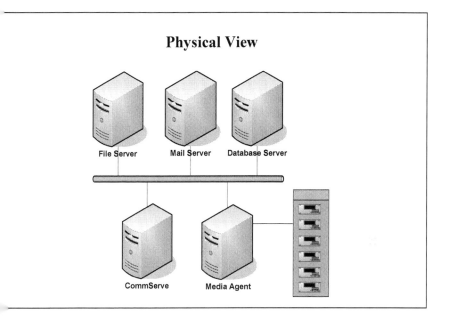

Results: Designating drive resources in the auxiliary copy options can ensure that if resources are available in the library that they will be used for the auxiliary copies. This is an alternative method to designating separated drive pools. The advantage here is that is no auxiliary copies are running at the time the drives can be used for regular backup jobs. If all drives are being used for backups the auxiliary copies will have to wait for drives to become available before they will be used. Note that once you configure the number of parallel streams for an auxiliary copy the setting can not be changed.

In-Line Encryption for Network and Data Security

Business Needs	• Provide encrypted backups for sensitive data • Encrypt data on clients for secure transmission of data over the network • Minimize performance impact of encrypting data
Infrastructure	• Several servers backing up over an unsecured network
CommVault® environment	• CommServe server, Media Agent and appropriate iDataAgent installed on each server
Solution	• Define separate subclients pointing to sensitive data • Configure subclients containing sensitive data to encrypt data at the client

Implementation: Encryption can be enabled at the client level. Settings such as encryption algorithm, bit length, and key management can be configured at this level.

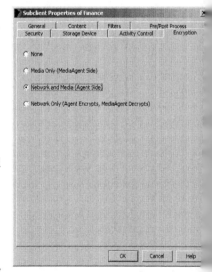

Encryption is then applied at the subclient level. This provides the flexibility to only encrypt data that needs to be. In this case by creating a subclient representing sensitive data and enabling encryption on that subclient, the sensitive data will be encrypted by the client and transmitted over the unsecured network. Data not requiring encryption will be defined in a different subclient and not encrypted thereby limiting the performance impact by only using encryption where it is needed.

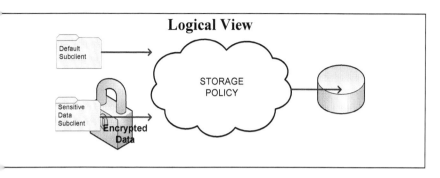

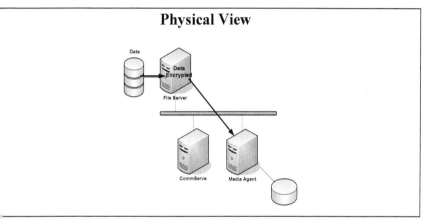

Results: When encrypting data over an unsecured link, using in-line encryption and selecting the option Network and Media Side allows data to be encrypted before it leaves the client. An additional option would be to Encrypt Network Only. Data will be encrypted on the Client and decrypted on the Media Agent. If the data needed to be restored it would then be encrypted on the Media Agent and Decrypted on the Client. In either case it is important to know that data will always be decrypted on the client side.

Off-Line Encryption for Data Security

Business Needs	• Protect data being sent off-site with encryption • Do not impact current performance for data protection operations • Minimize the impact on performance when performing auxiliary copy operations
Infrastructure	• Several file servers and an mail server • Disk and tape libraries
CommVault® environment	• CommServe server and a Media Agent • Tape library and magnetic library attached to the Media Agent
Solution	• Create subclients for sensitive data • Backup all production data to a magnetic library • Create a storage policy with a primary copy and 2 secondary copies • All non-sensitive data will be copied to a secondary copy with no encryption • All sensitive data will copied to a secondary copy with encryption enabled

Implementation: Data on production servers is divides into sensitive and non-sensitive subclients. This will allow the data to be managed independently in the backup environment. Data is backed up to a magnetic library unencrypted so no performance impact will occur. Then non-sensitive data is associated with a secondary copy with encryption turned off. Sensitive data will be directed to a secondary copy with encryption enabled. This limits the amount of data being encrypted reducing the impact on the Media Agent performing the encryption.

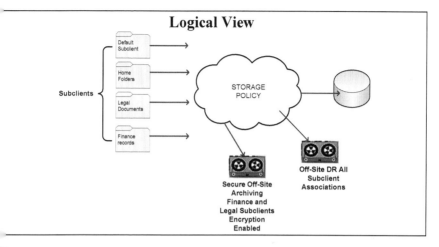

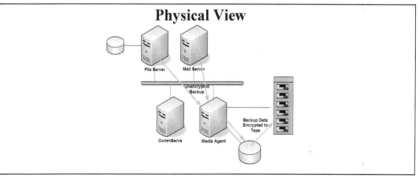

Results: CommVault software provides an efficient method of encrypting data by logically dividing sensitive data. Options for performing inline encryption where data can be encrypted over the network or to media can be used. In this case since data was being written to stationary magnetic media and network encryption was not needed, encryption could be performed when auxiliary copies were run. Using this method and logically dividing sensitive data minimized the impact of encrypting data.

Chapter 11

Distributed Environment Storage Policy Examples

Chapter Summary

- Distributed Storage Policy Design
- Consolidating backup Data Using Synthetic Fulls
- Performing Remote Backups Using USB Storage
- Multiple Backup Locations Using Multiple backup Sets

The following section provides examples on distributed environments using CommVault® solutions. The examples used focus on layout and storage policy design to meet the needs of organizations with many locations. Saying that, basic configurations such as retention and policy copies may not be part of the design examples. Basic storage policy configurations have already been covered in the basic and advanced design examples.

Distributed Environment Storage Policy Design

Business Needs	• Define local backup paths for distributed locations • Ensure data does not get directed over WAN connections during data protection • Centrally manage all backups from main datacenter
Infrastructure	• 5 locations each with dedicated datacenter and IT staff
CommVault® environment	• Central CommServe® server at main data center • Media Agents in each location with direct attached tape libraries
Solution	• Create five storage policies each defining a local data path

Implementation: Storage policies divide business data and define a data path. In this case 5 storage policies are created each defining a local data path.

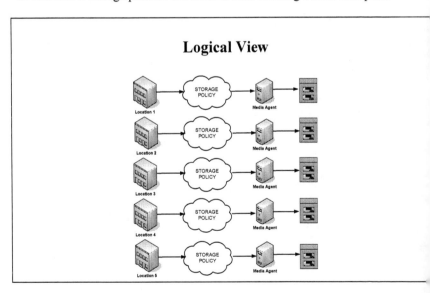

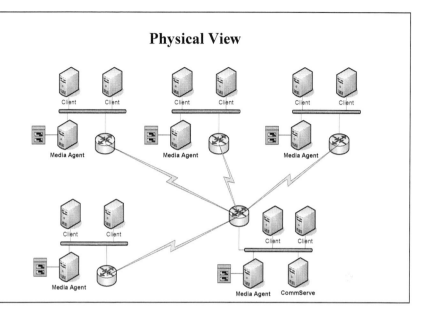

Physical View

Results: Defining local paths for each of the five locations results in all data being backed up to local libraries. In this case defining multiple storage policies ensures data will always take the appropriate path avoiding the WAN.

This also demonstrates how a distributed environment can be centrally managed. The CommServe system at the main location manages all locations. Backup administrators can access the CommServe through the CommCell® Console from any location as long as network connectivity and hostname resolution is established.

Consolidating Backup Data Using Synthetic Fulls

Business Needs	• Consolidate backup data by performing backups over WAN • Limit the amount of backup traffic over the WAN
Infrastructure	• 5 locations with adequate bandwidth to primary data center
CommVault® environment	• Agent software deployed to remote servers • CommServe server and Media Agent located at main datacenter
Solution	• Define a storage policy defining a data path to the Media Agent and library at the main datacenter • Schedule daily incrementals and weekly Synthetic Full backups

Implementation: This solution takes advantage of the Synthetic Full Feature. This feature synthesizes full backups by generating full copies from previous backup jobs. The result is that only incremental change data will be transmitted over the WAN.

A single storage policy is created directing remote data to the Media Agent and the library at the main datacenter. When scheduling backup operations, the option to use synthetic full is used. The default option to run an incremental before synthetic full ensures that the synthetic full will current as of the time the incremental was run.

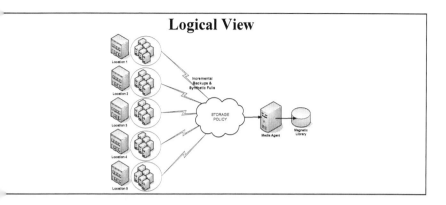

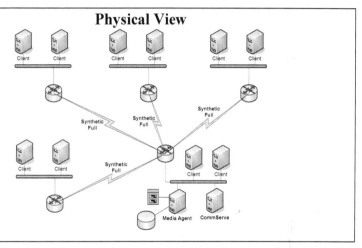

Results: Using synthetic fulls can greatly reduce the network bandwidth needed to backup data. In this case, by performing synthetic fulls over the WAN cuts down on bandwidth usage and allows for the consolidation of backup data at a centralized location.

NOTE: there are rules and limitations to the use of synthetic full operations. Refer to CommVault documentation for more information before implementing synthetic full operations.

Performing Remote Backups Using USB Storage Devices

Business Needs	• Provide backups at remote locations without the need for dedicated backup administrators • Design a media rotation scheme which will keep data at remote backup site and primary datacenter
Infrastructure	• Remote location with several file servers and a Media Agent
CommVault® environment	• Remote locations each have a Windows Server Media Agent • No tape libraries are being used
Solution	• Use USB storage drives to backup data • Rotate USB devices off-site to meet media rotation scheme

Implementation: Using USB storage devices can be an effective solution when protecting data at remote offices. A storage policy is created and the data path is defined to use a USB library. The USB storage is treated as a standalone tape library meaning that if the USB device is inserted into another Windows Media Agent the data can be recovered. This provides the ability to backup data at remote locations and restore the data at the main datacenter. To avoid USB key drives and smaller USB devices from being detected as a library you can specify the minimum size of a library that will be detected by CommVault software.

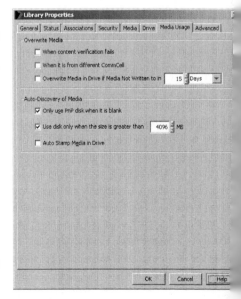

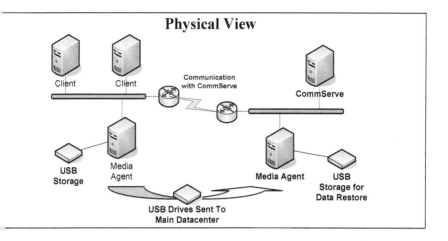

Results: Using USB disk drives to protect data can be a great advantage when backing up remote locations. Instead of purchasing a robotic tape library or relying on non-technical users to swap tapes in and out of drives, you can have them plug in a USB drive. Most people in this day and age will have the knowledge to plug a USB cable into a computer. Since USB drives are inexpensive and have a large capacity you can design a media rotation scheme to ensure on-site and off-site data are always available. USB storage devices can be plugged into any Windows Server Media Agent and restore from the server.

Multiple Backup Locations Using Synthetic Fulls and Multiple Backup Sets

Business Needs	• Backup data locally to SAN storage • Backup data over a WAN to the main datacenter where auxiliary copies will run to tape
Infrastructure	• Two data centers with SAN and Media Agents in each location
CommVault® environment	• CommServe server at main datacenter • Media Agents at each location
Solution	• Create two backup sets and two storage policies • Backup set Local will point to Storage Policy Local to backup data to the local SAN • Backup set Remote will point to Storage Policy Remote to backup data over the WAN • Implement daily incremental backups with weekly synthetic fulls

Implementation: By creating two backup sets you will have two logical views of data being protected. You create two storage policies each defining a different data path. Subclients within each backup set can be pointed to the proper storage policy so backups will run twice from the server each night. To reduce the load on the server when backing up twice incrementals will be performed nightly with minimal impact to the server and a weekly synthetic full will be run which will have no impact on the server.

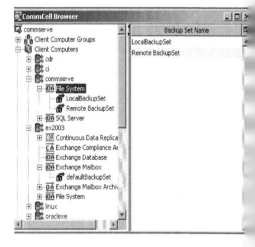

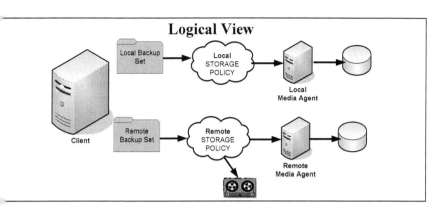

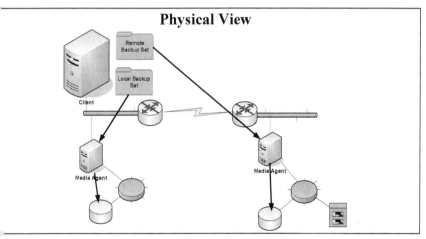

Results: Though it is not typically recommended to backup a system twice, this is an exception to the rule. In this situation data must be kept on-site for recovery but also sent off-site. Synthetic full operations only work on primary backup operations so performing a synthetic full locally and then using auxiliary copy over the WAN will saturate the WAN link. By performing incrementals and synthetic fulls twice, backup times will be short and the result will be a local and remote copy of all backup data.

Chapter 12

Enterprise Storage Policy Examples

Chapter Summary
- GridStor™ technology for failover, load balancing, and LAN-free backups
- Data path override
- Setting group permissions to secure data
- ILM storage policy strategy
- Using scratch pools for compliance copies

The following section illustrates methods to improve performance in backups within an enterprise environment. Using multiple Media Agents, GridStor™ technology, LAN-Free backups, and storage policy consolidation will be discussed.

Using GridStor™ Technology to Perform LAN-Free Backups

Business Needs	• Perform backups of database and file server without using the LAN
Infrastructure	• Database and file server SAN attached. • Data for both servers located on disk storage within the SAN
CommVault® environment	• CommServe® server • Media Agents and appropriate iDataAgents installed on both servers
Solution	• Installing Media Agent modules on each server will provide the processing to perform LAN free backups • A storage policy is created defining data paths for both media agent pointing to protected storage.

Implementation: When storage is directly attached to a server or if a server is attached to a SAN, LAN-Free backups can be used to avoid slower backups and saturation of the LAN. In this case the rule that all data must pass through a Media Agent results in placing a Media Agent module on each server. In the storage policy paths for both Media Agents will be defined. The Data Path Configuration will be configured to use the Preferred Path which represents the LAN-Free path.

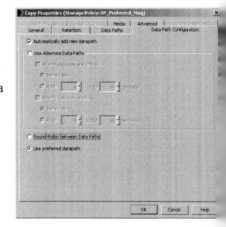

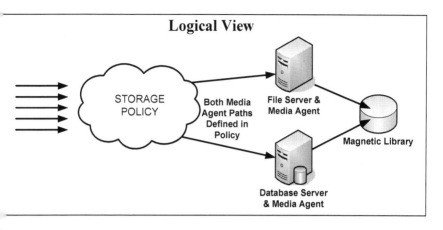

Logical View

STORAGE POLICY

Both Media Agent Paths Defined in Policy

File Server & Media Agent

Database Server & Media Agent

Magnetic Library

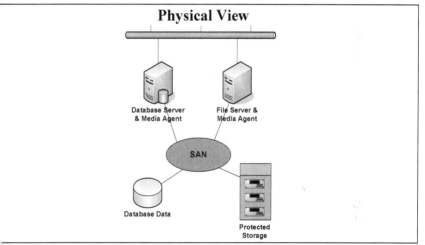

Physical View

Database Server & Media Agent

File Server & Media Agent

SAN

Database Data

Protected Storage

Results: installing Media Agent modules on any server that will perform LAN-free backups is required to avoid traffic over the LAN. The storage policy will be configured with two paths each defined for the two Media Agents. The storage policy will be configured to use *Default Path* providing the LAN-free solution.

Using GridStor™ Technology to Load Balance Backups

Business Needs	• Provide load balancing of file and application servers through two Media Agents to a Dynamic Drive Sharing Library
Infrastructure	• Servers with Direct Attached Storage (DAS) • SAN environment with a magnetic and tape library
CommVault® environment	• CommServe server and 2 SAN attached Media Agents
Solution	• Create a storage policy defining paths to both media agents • Configure the storage policy data paths to Load Balance between both paths

Implementation: Servers that will back up over the network can be load balanced between multiple Media Agents. This ensures a balanced load to each Media Agent being used. A storage policy is configured defining the data path to each Media Agent. Data path configuration options are then set to Round-Robin between data paths. Round robin load balancing will be performed on a job by job basis.

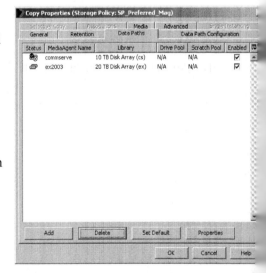

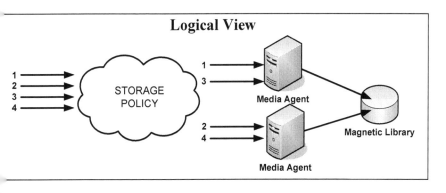

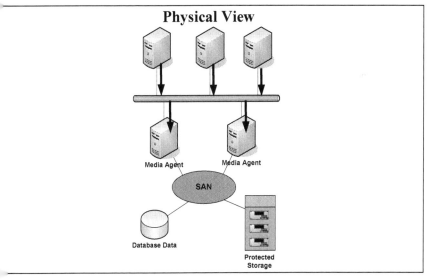

Results: Defining the storage policy to load balance is the most efficient way to backup servers with direct attached storage. As backups request storage resources Media Agents will be selected in a Round Robin fashion. It is important to note that entire backup jobs will be load balanced meaning that a multi-streamed job will send all streams to the same Media Agent.

Using GridStor™ Technology for Data Path Failover

Business Needs	• A critical server at a remote location must be backed up nightly. • The remote location does not have a dedicated IT staff and the company is worried about the success of backups if something goes wrong
Infrastructure	• Two locations with a WAN link connecting them
CommVault® environment	• CommServe server at main datacenter • Media Agents at both locations with direct attached tape libraries
Solution	• Create a storage policy with two paths one for each Media Agent at each location • Configure the storage policy to use the local Media Agent as the default path • Set the storage policy to failover to the other Media Agent if resources are offline

Implementation: Data path failover can ensure the successful completion of critical backup jobs in the event of a Media Agent or Library failure. In this case two paths are defined. the first path is the local path which will be marked as the default path. The second path will be defined to the remote backup location. The option to use alternate data paths will be set to When Resources are Offline and a wait of 2 hours will be set. This provides an opportunity to correct any problems before failover occurs. If the problem can not be fixed then the job will switch to the second path.

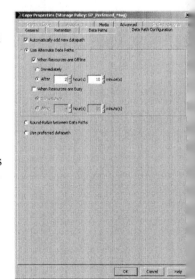

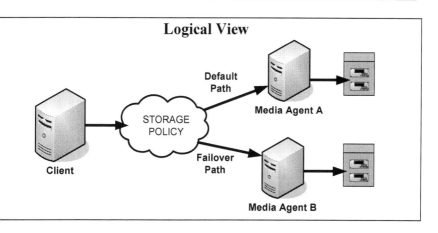

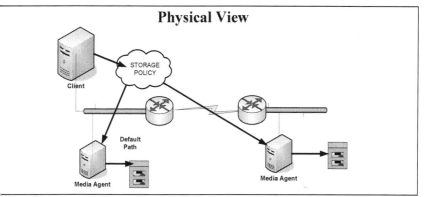

Results: Setting a storage policy with two paths configured to failover will allow for the client data to be backed up over the WAN only if the local Media Agent or library become unavailable. Off line failover can be configured to happen immediately or after a specified time. Consider setting a time range so you can be alerted and potentially fix the problem before failover will occur.

Consolidating Storage Policies Using Data Path Override

Business Needs	• Provide Round Robin load balancing for any LAN servers • Provide LAN free backup paths to SAN attached servers. Do not use these servers for load balancing LAN backups • Consolidate all data to media for off-site storage
Infrastructure	• High performance database and file server with large amounts of data in SAN environment • 2 file servers and a mail server with direct attached storage which will be backing up over the LAN
CommVault® environment	• 2 Media Agents used for load balancing • 2 dedicated Media Agents on a database servers and a file server
Solution	• Configure a storage policy with all required data paths defined • Use data path override option to force required subclient to only used appropriate paths

Implementation: Normally to accomplish the goal of load balancing LAN based backups but preventing them from using Media Agents installed on servers for the purpose of LAN-Free backups, two storage policies would be needed. One would be used for load balancing LAN backups and the other would use the Preferred Path option for LAN-Free backups.

Using the Data Path Override option in the subclient properties all subclients ca be directed to the same storage policy. For any LAN based backup operations the override will be set to only use the dedicated LAN Media Agents for load balancing. This prevents backup data from traveling through the Media Agents that are dedicated to performing LAN-Free operations. By using a single storag policy you will have the capability to combine data onto the same media allowing for better media management and data consolidation.

Logical View

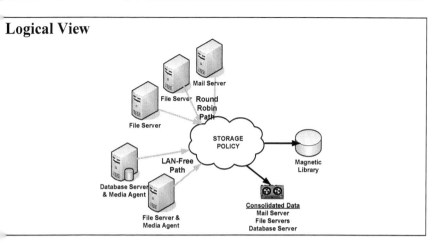

Physical View

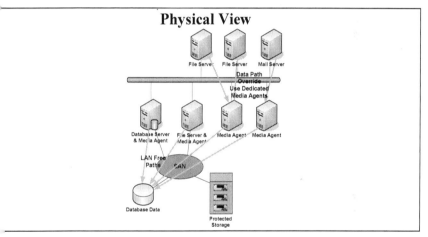

Results: Data path override is a powerful tool that allows you to designate specific paths that subclient data will take to storage. This does require more intricate configuration and adds a level of complexity into your backup environment. In this case the main advantage of using the data path override is to allow the consolidation of data on media and to avoid writing data through Media Agents that are designated to high performance servers.

Setting Permissions for Help Desk Group to Recover User Data

Business Needs	• Provide the ability for a dedicated help desk group to recover user data • Prevent help desk group from recovering sensitive financial records on the file server
Infrastructure	• File server with home folders and financial records data
CommVault® environment	• CommServe server • Media Agents and appropriate iDataAgents installed on both servers

Solution	• Create a help desk user group
	• Create 2 dedicated subclients
	  o Home folders
	  o Finance

Implementation: 2 subclients are created allowing each one to be managed separately. The help desk user group will be associated with the home folders subclient. This will allow members of the help desk group to recover ONLY data residing within the home folders subclient.

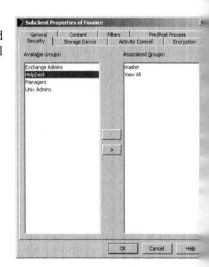

Logical View

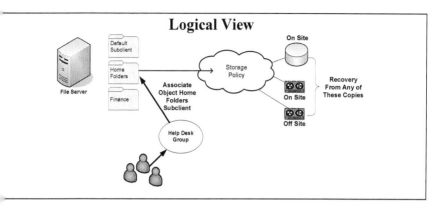

Results: For larger environments with many users accessing CommVault software it is essential to design a strong security policy. Data in the backup environment, if not properly protected, can become susceptible to compromise. In this case by creating a help desk group and associating them only with objects that they need to access, you restrict their ability to access sensitive information. This also illustrates another advantage of logically dividing data into subclients in the production environment.

Designing Storage Policies for Information Lifecycle Management

Business Needs	• Design an *Information Lifecycle Management* strategy to for the following files and user groups:
	    o Finance group XLS and PDF files
	    o Legal group PDF and DOC files
	    o Engineering group CAD files
	• Set SLA's according to chart below				

Group	**Files**	Tier 1 Online	Tier 2 Online	Tier 3 24 hours	Tier 4 5 days
Finance	XLS PDF	2 yrs	2 yrs	7 yrs	Infinite
Legal	PDF DOC	3 yrs	3 yrs	4 yrs	15 yrs
Engineering	CAD	1 yr	3 yrs	7 yrs	20 yrs

CommVault® environment	• CommServe server and Media Agents • File System iDataAgents, File Archiving agents, and Data Classification Enabler
Solution	• Create 3 storage policies. • Each policy will have a primary copy to disk and 2 copies to tape all with retention set to match SLA based on group • Define 3 DCE subclients 1 for each group. Associate the appropriate files and archiving rules to match SLA

Implementation: At first view of the SLA chart and the storage policy implementation diagram, it might appear that the numbers don't match up but they do. Tier 1 defines how long data must remain in the production environment. Archiving rules will be set to archive

data older then tier 1 SLA. At this point when data is archived, 3 copies of the data will be created. The primary copy to disk will be tier 2. The retention will be based on the SLA chart. Tier 3 will represent the secondary copy to tape to be kept on-site. This provides recovery of data if tier 2 disks fail, and will provide SLA beyond the SLA defined in tier 2. Because of this, the tier 3 retention will be the combined SLA of tier 2 and tier 3. The same will hold true for tier 4. Tier 4 is sent off-site for long term archiving and to provide DR protection in the case of site disaster.

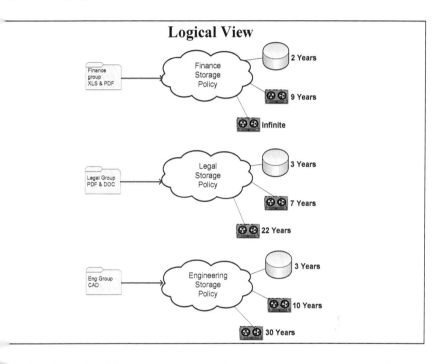

Logical View

Finance group XLS & PDF → Finance Storage Policy → 2 Years / 9 Years / Infinite

Legal Group PDF & DOC → Legal Storage Policy → 3 Years / 7 Years / 22 Years

Eng Group CAD → Engineering Storage Policy → 3 Years / 10 Years / 30 Years

Results: Archiving data provides a tremendous advantage for managing data throughout its useful lifecycle. The flexibility of Data Classification allows the intelligent management of data based on specific file attributes and ownership of those files. Storage policies allow different SLA's to be set for business needs. The integration of all of these components together makes the process of implementing an ILM system much easier then using third party systems.

Defining a Scratch Pool for Compliance Backups to Specific Media

Business Needs	• Provide the ability to generate copies of data on demand using a specific tape • Provide compliance backup data for auditors when requested
Infrastructure	• Several servers with sensitive data required to be archived on demand when requested by auditors
CommVault® environment	• CommServe server and Media Agent with direct attached library
Solution	• Create a compliance scratch pool in the library • When an auditor requests data and provides a tape add the tape, discover it, and move it to the compliance scratch pool • Create a secondary copy for compliance jobs and associate subclients when data is requested by auditors

Implementation: A scratch pool is defined for the tape library called Compliance. This pool will have no media associated with it. When specific requests come in to place certain data on a particular tape the tape is moved into the compliance scratch pool. A special storage policy copy will be created within the storage policy. When a compliance job is requested the data which will already exist in the backup environment can be copied to the secondary copy by associating the proper subclients with the secondary copy. The job is then run through an auxiliary copy operation. The result will be the jobs are written to the specific media moved into the compliance scratch pool.

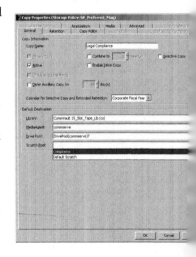

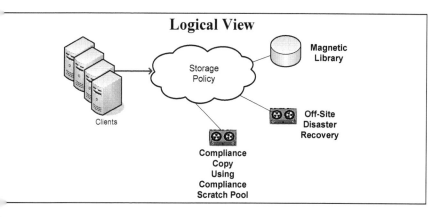

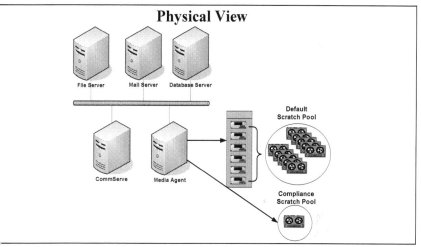

Results: Compliance issues can cause problems in an environment by making special requests for specific data. By logically grouping data into subclients in anticipation of such requests and designating a specific scratch pool to place special media, you can be prepared and simplify the process.

Chapter 13

Storage Policy Design for Disaster Recovery

Chapter Summary
- Meeting recovery point objectives
- Meeting recovery time objectives
- Job placement on media for prioritized recovery
- Configuring backups for CommServe® database
- Encrypting CommServe database backups

The following section provides real world solutions to prepare for recovery in the event of a disaster. Close attention should be paid to day-to-day operations of backups to prepare for a disaster. Without strong preparation, all your work of managing your backup data may be for nothing if you didn't consider how protecting your data may impact your ability to recover it.

Defining Production Data to Meet Recovery Point Objectives

Business Needs	<ul><li>Provide protection for a critical orders database</li><li>Meet a RPO of 30 minutes for the database with on-site and off-site copies of transaction log data</li></ul>
Infrastructure	<ul><li>Database server</li><li>2 locations with magnetic disk storage at each</li><li>Adequate bandwidth for WAN backups</li></ul>
CommVault® environment	<ul><li>CommServe® server and Media Agent with direct attached disk storage at main location</li><li>Media Agent with direct attached disk storage at remote location</li></ul>
Solution	<ul><li>Create a subclient for the orders database</li><li>Schedule regular backups of database once a day</li><li>Schedule transaction log backups to run every 30 minutes</li><li>Create a storage policy with 2 copies<ul><li>Primary to disk at main location</li><li>Secondary to disk at remote location associated with the orders subclient</li></ul></li><li>Configure auxiliary copy to use automatic copy. Set interval to 30 minutes</li></ul>

Implementation: Critical databases can be defined as subclients. Some database subclients provide the flexibility of directing fulls and differentials to one storage policy and transaction logs to another. If the database iDataAgent does not provide this flexibility you can still use incremental storage policies to accomplish this goal.

Transaction log backups being smaller then fulls or differentials can be run more frequently. In this case to meet the Recovery Point Objective of 30 minutes, transaction log backups will be scheduled to run every half hour. This will protect the data but an off-site copy is also required. Creating a secondary copy and using the automatic auxiliary copy feature to run on half hour intervals will allow the copy to update itself as new transaction log backups are run. This accomplishes the on-site and off-site 30 minute RPO goal.

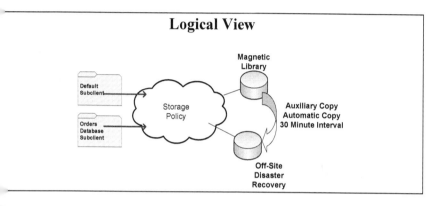

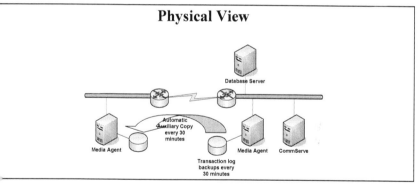

Results: For some organizations meeting goals such as this would result in using disk replication. Replication is expensive but very effective at meeting short RPO's. By scheduling 30 minute transaction log backups and using the automatic auxiliary copy feature you can meet your RPO goals without investing in dedicated hardware or software. This also protects a backup of data which can be beneficial in the event that production data becomes corrupt

Defining Production Data to Meet Recovery Time Objectives

Business Needs	• Managers and Executives must have a RTO of 4 hours for e-mail • Users will have a 24 hour RTO
Infrastructure	• Mail server with a separate mail store database for managers and executive and a separate database for regular users
CommVault® environment	• CommServe server and Media Agent • Appropriate file system and mail application iDataAgents installed on mail server
Solution	• Define a separate subclient for executives and managers e-mail

Implementation: By logically dividing data into subclients the data can be restored separately. In this case the executives and managers e-mail can be recovered as a separate job. This does require the executives and managers mailboxes be stored in a different database then other users.

Logical View

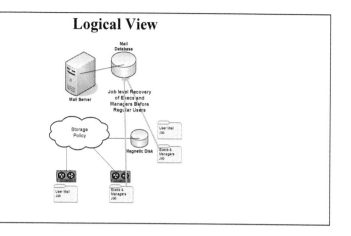

Physical View

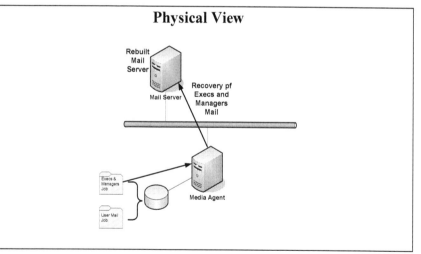

Results: This example illustrates how Recovery Time Objectives should be based on business systems. By logically grouping data into subclients, you can recover different information at different times. If the overall size of the all e-mail was 800GB but the executives and managers e-mail size was 100GB, dividing the data results in a shorter point to recover the prioritized data. In this case it is quicker to restore 100GB of data then all 800GB.

Job Placement on Storage for Prioritized Recovery of Critical Servers

Business Needs	• Provide a prioritized recovery of 8 critical servers • Be able to recover the 4 top priority servers at the same time
Infrastructure	• Primary datacenter with 8 drive library • DR site with a 4 drive library
CommVault® environment	• CommServe server and Media Agent • Appropriate iDataAgents installed on all 8 critical servers
Solution	• Create a storage policy with 4 secondary copies • The top 4 priority servers will be associated with a different secondary copy forcing each server backup to different media • Server priorities 5-8 will also be associated with the 4 secondary copies

Implementation: In this case, the placement of jobs on media is very important. If the top four priority servers are all on the same tape, they can only be recovered one at a time. By creating a storage policy with four copies and moving each of the top four priority servers to their own copy ensures that they can all be recovered at the same time using the four drive library at the DR facility. Priority servers five through eight can then be recovered once the top priority servers are restored.

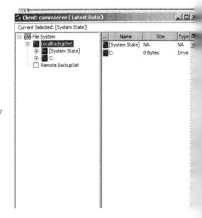

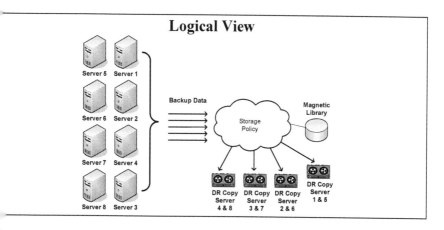

Logical View

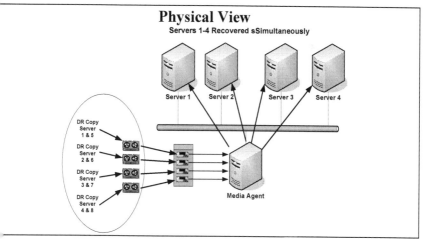

Physical View
Servers 1-4 Recovered sSimultaneously

Results: By creating different copies representing priorities in recovery you can match the number of servers to recovery simultaneously based on the number of drives in your DR site.

DR Backup Solution with Dedicated Storage Policy

Business Needs	• Provide a DR strategy for protecting the CommServe database • Ensure the CommServe database is on its own tape
Infrastructure	• Main datacenter and DR facility
CommVault® environment	• CommServe server at main datacenter • Standby CommServe system at DR site
Solution	• Configure DR backup settings to use a dedicated DR storage policy

Implementation: When the first library in a CommCell® environment is created a DR storage policy is automatically set up. By default every day at 10AM a DR backup is performed. The first phase exports the CommServe database, registry settings, and any firewall configuration files to a network share. The second phase takes the exported data and writes through the designated storage policy to media. The DR backup settings in Control Panel allow you to configure which storage policy to use. Since storage policies create logical divisions of data the goal of isolating DR backups onto dedicated media is accomplished.

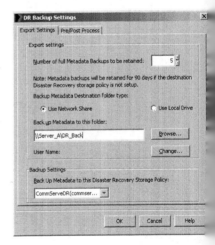

Logical View

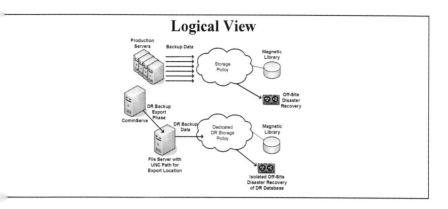

Physical View

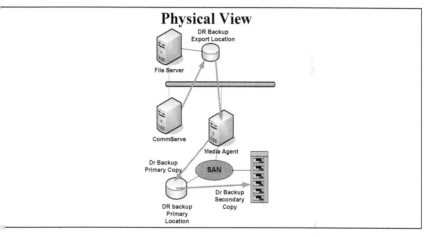

Results: Using a dedicated DR storage policy allows you to isolate DR backups on media. This can be an advantage when using custom barcode labels and you want to easily identify which tape the DR backup is on. Consider however that if you are shipping tapes off-site everyday that the DR backup should be sent off-site as well. Isolating DR backups on their own media can be a good thing but it will require a lot of underutilized media being sent off-site. If your DR database is 500 MB in size and you are writing it to an 800GB capacity tape you will wasting a lot of space. The next example shows you how to integrate DR backups with regular backup data.

CommServe Database Backup Solution Using a Shared Storage Policy

Business Needs	• Provide a DR strategy for protecting the CommServe database
	• Provide off-site storage of CommServe database
	• Consolidate the number of media being sent off-site
Infrastructure	• Main datacenter and DR facility
CommVault® environment	• CommServe server at main datacenter
	• Standby CommServe system at DR site
Solution	• Configure the Dr backup settings to us a normal backup storage policy for DR backups

Implementation: By default the DR backup will use a dedicated storage policy. Though this is good to isolate DR backups on media it requires separate media to manage backup data and DR data. By associating the DR backup to a regular storage policy you accomplish the goal of consolidating the number of media being sent off-site. Ensure that you are running and protecting job reports so you can use the reports to determine what tape the DR backup is on.

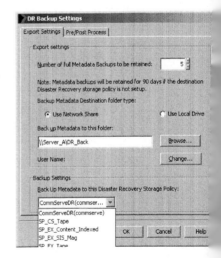

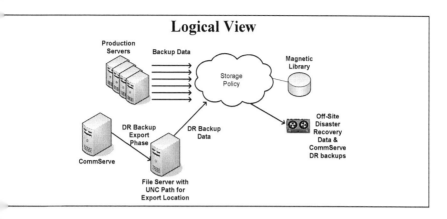

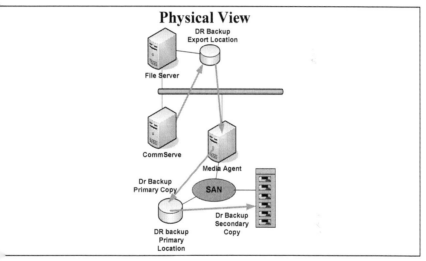

esults: Associating the DR backup with a regular storage policy is not a
ommVault best practice. However when it comes to saving media and money
is can be an effective solution. Always ensure that you run and redundantly
ore reports and that you will have access to these reports in a disaster situation.
heck with CommVault and documentation and professional services for more
formation on preparing for a disaster using CommVault solutions.

Encrypting CommServe Database Backups

Business Needs	• Provide off-site storage of CommServe database • Ensure that the CommServe database is encrypted before sending off-site
Infrastructure	• Main datacenter and DR facility
CommVault® environment	• CommServe server at main datacenter • Standby CommServe system at DR site
Solution	• Associate the CommServe database backup with a storage policy • Configure a secondary copy and enable encryption on that copy

Implementation: By default DR backups are not encrypted. By using the off-line encryption feature you can create a secondary copy and enable encryption for that copy. The storage policy primary copy should be maintained on-site and secure. The encrypted secondary copy can be sent off-site.

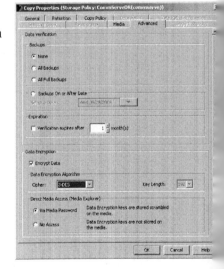

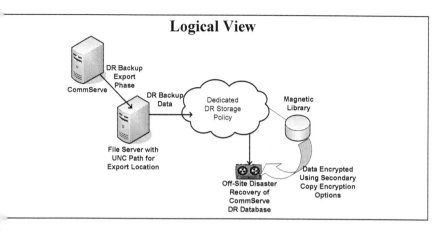

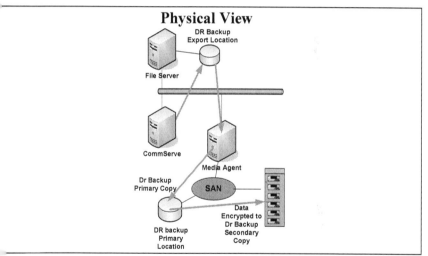

Results: The CommServe database is the central repository for all CommCell environment information. It is absolutely critical it is properly protected. Not only does it store all metadata regarding the CommCell environment but it also maintains encryption keys. If someone could get a copy of the DR database they could possibly gain access to all backup data even if it is being encrypted. This solution allows you to properly protect and encrypt the DR database.

Glossary

Alternate data path
Combination of Media Agent, Library , Drive Pool and Scratch Pool which are added to a Storage Policy as an alternate data path, so that an alternate resource can be used for data protection operations, when a component in the default data path is not available.

Auxiliary copy operation
Copies the backup data that was created on a primary copy to all auxiliary copies within the storage policy.

Backup Set
A group of subclients which includes all of the data backed up by the iDataAgent.

Basic retention rule
A feature used to define the retention rules for data in days and cycles.

Client
A computer in a CommCell that has agent software installed on it.

CommCell® architecture
The basic organizational unit of a data management system. A CommCell environment contains one CommServe® Storage Manager, at least one client, and at least one Media Agent.

CommCell® Console
The graphical user interface used to access and manage the system.

CommServe® server
The software module that communicates with all clients and Media Agents and coordinates operations (data protection, data recovery, and administration operations, job management, event management, etc.) within a CommCell environment. There is only one CommServe server within a CommCell architecture.

Content Indexing
A feature used to search archived data of supported file and message types by its content.

Data aging
Operation that logically deletes expired data based on storage policy copy retention.

Data encryption
The software uses asymmetrical encryption. The plaintext is encrypted with one key (called public), and can be decrypted only with the other key (called private). The software uses public key encryption to avoid prompting for a pass-phrase each time a backup runs.

Data multiplexing
A feature that allows data from multiple clients/subclients to be written to the same drive/media, when a set of data protection operations are running concurrently.

Data stream
A data channel through which client data flows to a backup media.

Differential backup
A backup of all of the data of a subclient that has changed since the subclient's last full backup.

Disaster Recovery
The planning for and/or the implementation of a strategy to respond to such failures as a total infrastructure loss, or the failure of computers (CommServe server, Media Agent, client, or application), networks, storage hardware, or media. A Disaster Recovery strategy typically involves the creation and maintenance of a secure Disaster Recovery site, and the day-to-day tasks of running regular Disaster Recovery backups.

Disaster Recovery Backup
Backs up meta data and Windows registry data during two phases. The export phase backs up the data to a local or network path and the backup phase backs

up the data to media using an Disaster Recovery Backup storage policy. This data can then be restored using the CommServe Recovery Tool.

Disaster Recovery Backup storage policy
A storage policy used to store metadata to media. This metadata stores information about the CommCell environment and the backed up data. In case of a system failure, Disaster Recovery Backup data can be retrieved using this storage policy.

Drive pool
Logical entities used to facilitate the sharing of a library's drives between multiple Media Agents.

Extended retention rules
A feature used to define an extended retention time and days exceeding basic retention rules

Full backup
A backup of all of the data of a subclient. A full backup provides the baseline for subsequent incremental and differential backups. (Known as a level 0 backup in Oracle.)

Incremental backup
A backup of all of the data of a subclient that has changed since the subclient's last full, incremental, or differential backup.

Information Lifecycle Management
Concept of managing data based on file ownership and file type throughout it's useful lifecycle.

Intelligent Data Agent (iDataAgent)
A software module that backs up and restores data of a particular application type on a host computer system.

Job Controller
The window in the CommCell Console which can be used to monitor and manage the active jobs in the CommCell.

Library
A storage unit that contains a robotic device, one or more media drives, and multiple media cartridges for extended storage capacity. Within the CommCell Console all storage devices are referred to as libraries.

Magnetic library
Configuration where DAS, NAS, or SAN disk is configured as a library to backup data to disk.

Migration archiving
An operation which moves data from a client computer to secondary storage media, for the purpose of reducing costs associated with backing up and maintaining the data on primary storage.

Network Agent
A feature which can be used to increase the data transfer throughput from a client during data protection operations.

Network bandwidth throttling
A feature which can be used to control the amount of data transferred in a network during a data protection operation.

On Demand Backup Set / Archive Set
A logical entity that allows data to be backed up or archived through a Directive File specified at the point of backup/archive. The Directive File contains the fully qualified path(s) to one or more Content Files which contain the fully qualified path(s) to one or more files, links and/or devices to be backed up. For some agents a single Content File is used in place of the Directive File.

Primary copy
The logical entity in a storage policy through which all data protection operations are conducted.

Recovery Point Objective (RPO)
The point in time in which protected data must be recovered to.

Recovery Time Objective (RTO)
The allotted time to recover a business system after a disaster in order to resume business operations

Scratch pool
A repository for new or pruned media which are available for use.

Selective copy
The logical entity in a storage policy used by an auxiliary copy operation to copy full backups that meet the specified criteria, from the primary copy.

Service Level Agreement (SLA)
Formally agreed upon service time for business system accessibility or data availability.

Single-instancing of data
A data storage approach that stores only a single copy of a file in a pool of storage. For example, content addressable storage (CAS) systems.
The software supports this operation by writing the data in a single-instanceable format for appliances that support single instancing of data.

Storage policy
A logical entity through which data from a subclient is backed up. A storage policy consists of one or more copies which associate data with particular physical media.

Storage policy copy
A logical entity which provides the path to the backup data and also provides the facility to define the retention period for the data.

subclient
The logical entity that uniquely defines a unit of data on a client computer.

Synchronous copy
The logical entity in a storage policy used by auxiliary copy operation to copy backup data occurring on or after a selected date on the primary copy

Synthetic full backup
An operation that combines the most recent full backup of the selected data with all subsequent incremental/differential backups and stores the result in a single archive file.

Index

Training Services

CommVault® Training Services provide worldwide onsite and offsite training for CommVault® products. Packaged or customized training courses are available in instructor-led or computer based formats. With extensive hands-on methods, experienced instructors guide students through real-world applications of CommVault software modules. Behind-the-scenes product technology is explained and demonstrated while best practices are showcased.

CommVault® Training Philosophy

Most IT staffs are familiar with the basic concepts of data management and have various degrees of expertise with their current data management products. But CommVault's singe-platform architecture and software is truly unique and takes data management to a new and higher level. CommVault training is vital to help ensure efficient, effective use of all features and functionality of the CommVault product suite. It can mean the difference between struggling along as before and taking advantage of the differentiators that led you to choose CommVault in the first place.

Training or Installation First? You Decide.

Attending training before installation helps you hit the ground running letting you pay closer attention to the work that goes into the implementation. System configuration tasks such as storage policy design, data retention settings, and schedule policy creation are also much easier when you already know what you are doing.

On the other hand, with post-installation training, you already know what your installation actually looks like. The experience of the implementation process and issue confrontation enables you to ask more focused and pertinent questions in class, which can significantly increase the value of the training.

Clearly, there are advantages to both options. Choose whichever one best suits your needs and preferences.

http://www.commvault.com/training

CommVault® Training Environment

To effectively meet our customer's training requirements and to overcome any training facility hardware limitations, certain CommVault training uses a simulated data center through virtualization software with pre-configured virtual machines and devices. This environment allows each student to learn CommVault component installation, network configuration options, function and feature configuration, and job management in a simulated real world data center. This may include different file systems (Windows, Linux/UNIX, etc.), applications (Exchange, SQL, etc.), and removable media libraries in either a direct-attached or SAN-based configuration.

CommVault System Administration Course

Prerequisites

Attendees require an Administration level of understanding of Windows 2000/2003 Server.

Description

This course provides students with the knowledge and skills necessary for administration of users, tasks, clients, libraries, and media using the CommCell® Console interface for the CommVault Common Technology Engine (CTE). Practical examples and "Hands-on" labs are used to reinforce the concepts in this course such as:

- User administration and security
- Client and storage policy configuration
- Library and media management options
- Task management
- Restore procedures and options
- Overall system monitoring

While the most recent available version of the software is used in class, the presented concepts, procedures, and best practices are applicable to all supported versions.

http://www.commvault.com/training

CommVault System Engineering Course

Prerequisites
Attendees must have attended the CommVault System Administration course.

Description
This course provides students with the knowledge and skills necessary for planning and design, installation, performance tuning and troubleshooting the CommVault Common Technology Engine (CTE). Practical examples and "Hands-on" labs are used to reinforce the concepts in this course such as:

> ➢ Planning the CommVault environment
> ➢ Best practices for installation of software components and device configuration
> ➢ Tools for problem analysis and performance tuning
> ➢ Successful troubleshooting methodologies

While the most recent available version of the software is used in class, the presented concepts, procedures, and best practices are applicable to all supported versions.

CommVault System Support Course

Prerequisites
Attendees must have attended the CommVault System Administration course.

Description
This course provides students with the knowledge and skills necessary for supporting customers and field engineers in the installation and operation of the CommVault Common Technology Engine (CTE). Practical examples,

in depth product process reviews, and "Hands-on" labs are used to reinforce the concepts in this course such as:

> ➢ Common problems and solutions for installation of software components and device configuration
> ➢ Tools for problem analysis and performance tuning
> ➢ Successful troubleshooting methodologies

While the most recent available version of the software is used in class, the presented concepts and best practices are applicable to all supported versions.

CommVault Archiving and Content Indexing Administration

Prerequisites:
Attendees require an Administration level of understanding of Windows 2000/2003 Server

Description
This course provides students with the knowledge and skills necessary for administration of compliance archiving, migration archiving, content indexing, and search using the CommCell® Console interface for the CommVault Common Technology Engine (CTE). Practical examples and "Hands-on" labs are used to reinforce the concepts in this course such as:

> ➢ Installation, configuration, and administration of migration archiving for Exchange, SharePoint, Domino E-mail and Network Appliance File Server
> ➢ Installation, configuration, and administration of compliance archiving for Exchange
> ➢ Recalling/Recovering of archived data
> ➢ Sizing and installing a content indexing engine
> ➢ Configuration and administration of Online and Offline content indexing
> ➢ Installation, configuration, and administration of compliance and end-user search interfaces

➢ Accessing/restoring search results
➢ Archiving, Content Indexing, and Search best practices

While the most recent available version of the software is used in class, the presented concepts and best practices are applicable to all supported versions starting with version 7.0.

Course includes an e-learning CD for end-user search training

CommVault Disaster Recovery Course

Prerequisites
Attendees require an Administration level of understanding of Windows 2000/2003 Server.

Description
This course provides students with the knowledge and skills necessary for recovering from a disaster at all levels using the CommVault Common Technology Engine (CTE). Practical examples and "Hands-on" labs are used to reinforce the concepts in this course such as reducing risks, recovering CommCell® components, and recovering an application server. While the course uses the most recent available version of the software, the presented concepts and best practices are applicable to all supported versions.

CommVault Self-Paced eLearning Modules

CommVault Educational Services self-paced eLearning modules cover many topics and features That though important, do not necessarily warrant or require a full instructor led classroom implementation. These self-paced courses are broken down into short, succinct online modules with:

- Topic Overviews that explain the purpose, functionality, and benefits of the product or feature covered
- Explanations of specific terms, processes, and configurations
- Demonstrations of configuration, monitoring, and other tasks
- You also get all the benefits inherent to all self-paced learning including:
  - No travel or extended time away from the office
  - You define the training schedule as the training is always ready when you are
  - You can review topics as often as you like

CommVault Help Desk Administration

Are your System Administrators handling Help Desk issues? So why not free-up your System Administrators by arming your Help Desk Administrators with the tools they need to recover lost files and user panic attacks?
This interactive, self-paced, CD-based course teaches Help Desk Administrators how to   deliver top-notch, help desk support using CommVault Galaxy® to restore files and e-mail messages.

The curriculum includes:

- The Galaxy architecture—including policy-based storage management concepts
- Step-by-step instructions for how to perform backups and restores
- Step-by-step instructions for how to manage and monitor Galaxy services
- Methods for configuring Galaxy reports

1-Touch

This self-paced, CD-based eLearning module is a 40 minute lesson that describes and demonstrates:

- ➢ 1-Touch Windows/Unix/Linux System Requirements
- ➢ Installation
- ➢ Client Configuration
- ➢ 1-Touch System Recovery
- ➢ 1-Touch Best Practices

CommNet™ Service Manager

This self-paced, CD-based eLearning module is a 45 minute lesson that describes and demonstrates:

- ➢ What is a CommNet™ environment
- ➢ Registering and Configuring CommCells or QSM Cells
- ➢ Setting up Alerts
- ➢ Billing and Cost
- ➢ Comprehensive Reports
- ➢ Monitoring Jobs and Resources

Continuous Data Replicator (CDR)

This self-paced, CD-based eLearning module is a 1 hour lesson that describes and demonstrates:

- ➢ What CDR is
- ➢ CDR Installation
- ➢ CDR Configuration
- ➢ CDR Operations
- ➢ And CDR Best Practices

CommVault Web Search End User Training

This self-paced, CD-based eLearning module is a 20 to 30 minute lesson intended for non-administrative CommVault Web Search end users. This module describes and demonstrates:

> ➤ CommVault Content Indexing & Search Overview
> ➤ CommVault Web Search Console
> ➤ End User Search
> ➤ Compliance Search & Legal Hold

CommVault Common Technology Engine (CTE) Desktop Quick Reference

All CommVault Simpana software products use the Common Technology Engine (CTE) architecture. This architecture is the world's only scalable framework optimized for data management. The CTE provides a common set of services for use by all CommVault products, including secure data movement, a common management console interface, and shared device management.

This quick reference provides fast answers to what features and functionality makes up the CTE and what they do. New and experienced CommVault Administrators will find this handy reference invaluable when installing, configuring, or using the CTE.

Table of Contents

Note: As always, the definitive guide to CommVault's Common Technology Engine and product suite is the latest version of CommVault's Online Books available, which can be found at http://documentation.commvault.com.

CommVault® Certification Program

CommVault's new certification program validates expertise and advanced knowledge in CommVault Administration, Implementation, and Support. The certification assessment and recognition is included with the relevant training course at no extra charge. Previous CommVault students who have attended class on or after July 1, 2005 may also be certified for free through an online assessment.

CommVault® Certification Program — Assessment Exams

Certification exam(s) are available online to the individual student upon completion of the course. A 75% comprehension level is required to successfully pass the assessment exam(s). Details on how the online assessment exams are accessed will be provided by the instructor during the course. All students who fully participate in an instructor-led course receive a "Certificate of Completion." Students successfully completing the assessment exam receive an additional "Certificate of Excellence" and their certification achievement is recorded as part of their student registration profile.

Key Points

- ➢ Certification is integrated with and managed through CommVault's Online Registration system.
- ➢ Cost of certification registration is included in the associated training course.
- ➢ Students may take the online certification exam(s) any time after completing the course.
- ➢ Previous training course students (as validated by the registrar) can also request an opportunity to take the online assessment exam at no charge.
- ➢ For those that feel they do not require training, an online assessment opportunity for each certification level may be purchased separately from the training course.

http://www.commvault.com/training

> ➤ You will only be allowed a single exam session so you must complete the entire exam at once without closing your browser. Please make sure that you have 90 minutes of uninterrupted time set aside to take the exam.
> ➤ You must have pop-ups enabled as the exam is launched in its own browser window.
> ➤ If you have registered for an exam only, please allow 1-3 business days for us to confirm your registration for this exam. Once your exam has been confirmed, you will then be able to access and take the exam.
> ➤ You will receive your certificates for all passing exams within 2-3 weeks.

CommVault® Certification Program — Certification Levels

CommVault Certified for Administration

To become CommVault Certified for Administration you must have attended a CommVault System Administration course and successfully passed the associated assessment exam. The exam assesses the candidate's level of comprehension for:

> ➤ Basic user and system administration tasks for secure data management
> ➤ Configuration and management of storage policies, data retention, and protection options for protecting data
> ➤ Configuration and role of agents, data sets, and subclients in defining protected data requirements
> ➤ Understanding data movement and storage options with various types of libraries and media
> ➤ Scheduling, executing, and managing jobs for protecting and recovering data
> ➤ Management of media both inside and outside of libraries
> ➤ Options for restoration and recovery of data, systems, and applications

http://www.commvault.com/training

CommVault Certified for Engineering

To become CommVault Certified for Engineering you must have attended both a CommVault System Administration course and a CommVault Engineering course, and successfully passed the associated assessment exams. The Engineering exam assesses the candidate's level of comprehension for:

> - Planning and designing a data management solution
> - Installation requirements and best practices for software components and libraries
> - Effective and proper use of available tools for identifying and resolving problems and performance
> - Identification of performance issues and options to improve performance
> - Understanding of common problems and solutions, and the methodology for identifying and resolving problems that may occur.

CommVault Certified for Support

To become CommVault Certified for Support you must have attended both a CommVault System Administration course and a CommVault Support course, and successfully passed the associated assessment exams. The Support exam assesses the candidate's level of comprehension for:

> - Installation requirements and best practices for software components and libraries
> - Effective and proper use of available tools for identifying and resolving problems and performance
> - Identification of performance issues and options to improve performance
> - Understanding of component services, communications, and processes used in execution of tasks
> - Understanding of common problems and solutions, and the methodology for identifying and resolving problems that may occur

CommVault Certified Specialist

The CommVault Certified Specialist - Archiving & Content Indexing Online Exam assesses the candidate's level of comprehension for:

> - Installation, configuration, and administration of migration archiving
> - Installation, configuration, and administration of compliance archiving
> - Recalling/Recovering of archived data
> - Sizing and installing a content indexing engine
> - Configuration and administration of Online and Offline content indexing
> - Installation, configuration, and administration of compliance and end-user search interfaces
> - Accessing/restoring search results
> - Archiving, Content Indexing, and Search best practices

Made in the USA
Lexington, KY
16 June 2011